BUSHELS of CRAFTS

101 Exciting New Projects for Children
at Church • VBS • Day Camp • Clubs • School • Home

Compiled by Christy Weir

The patterns in this book may be reproduced.

Printed in U.S.A.
Library of Congress Cataloging in Publication Data

Weir, Christy.
    Bushels of crafts.

    "The ideas for this craftbook were contributed by:
Barbara Colbert . . . [et al.]"—P. [4] of cover.
    1. Handicraft—Study and teaching (Elementary)
I. Thimsen, Joyce. II. Colbert, Barbara. III. Title
TT150.W45   1987   745.5   86-25652
ISBN 0-8307-1196-1

ISBN 0-8307-1196-1

Contents

Crafts Can Teach

"Crafts are for . . .

   . . . keeping kids busy!

      . . . giving them something to take home.

         . . . using up a lot of throw-away materials.

            . . . helping children learn."

While all of the above are true to a point, the last statement is the focus of this article.

Crafts can be a means of helping children learn many things, such as:

"Mandy doesn't like having her face spattered with paint."

   "Fake fur tickles!"

      "Three out of four of our glue bottles are clogged."

         "Not all marking pens wash off."

           "Ramon won't share the scissors!"

  Useful information like that.

And more besides. Some people use craft projects to help children learn about—

- finishing what they start
- developing their artistic capacities
- working well with others
- using materials wisely
- handling satisfaction over a good achievement
- handling frustration over a "failed" project.

Children do need to learn those things.

But crafts can also help reinforce Bible learning, by giving a child something physical to do as an expression of something heard in a Bible story.

And the Bible verse depicted on a craft project can repeatedly bring those important words back to a child's thinking.

Such learning is important and is the main reason for this book. You'll find a wide variety of project ideas to use with children from age two through eleven.

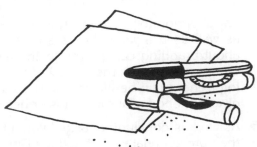

And most of them are easily adaptable to help you reinforce whatever Bible lesson you want to be sure is not forgotten.

Turn the page to see some examples of how crafts really can support Bible learning.

Stimulating Bible Learning Through Crafts

1. When you select a project, think carefully of how you might relate it to your teaching purpose. Even though every description in this book may not deal specifically with your lesson, a little thought can usually bring to mind several ideas of how to make a connection. For example, the "Prayer Calendar" activity is pictured with the words "I will be faithful to pray for others." If your lesson focuses on Creation, the wording on the frame could simply be changed to "Thank you God for your creation" or "Look what God has made."

2. When you introduce the craft, start by explaining its purpose in regard to Bible learning, not just its practical function. For example, the "Peaceful Hand Memo Holder" will serve as a place to keep a note pad. But its purpose is to remind children to use their hands in peaceful ways. Introduce the activity by saying, **Today you will make a note holder that will remind you to act peacefully toward others.**

3. As children work, be conscious of your role as teacher, not just as craft instructor. While much of your attention will need to be given to helping children complete the project successfully, look for moments to slip in a question about the craft's teaching purpose. Most of the projects in this book have "Conversation Suggestions" to help stimulate your thinking of appropriate questions to ask or comments to offer.

4. Pay attention to the interaction among children as well as the work they are doing. A lesson about bragging can be put to the test as children notice each other's work. Or a lesson on forgiveness can be illustrated when a child forgives a friend for bumping his or her arm.

5. As work is concluding, ask children to tell how their project relates to that day's Bible learning. Ask questions such as: **What will this help you remember about (peace)? How can you use this to show that you have learned about (peace)? What could you say about this craft to (a friend, your parents, etc.) that would help explain what you've learned?**

Preparing to Do Crafts

- **If you are planning to use crafts with a child at home, here are three helpful tips:**

1. Focus on the projects in the section for your child's age, but don't ignore projects that are listed for older or younger ages. Elementary aged children enjoy many of the projects grouped under "Crafts for Young Children" and they can do them with little or no adult assistance. And younger children are always interested in doing "big kid" things. Just plan on working along with the child, helping with tasks the child cannot handle alone.

2. Start with projects which call for materials you have around the house. Make a list of items you do not have which are needed for projects you think your child will enjoy. Plan to gather those supplies in one expedition.

3. If certain materials seem too difficult to obtain, a little thought can usually lead to appropriate substitutions. And often the homemade version ends up being a real improvement over the original plan.

- **If you are planning to lead a group of children in doing craft projects, keep these hints in mind:**

1. Choose projects which will allow children to work with a variety of materials.

2. Make your selection of all projects far enough in advance of need to allow time to gather all needed supplies in one coordinated effort. Many projects use some of the same items.

3. Make up a sample of each project to be sure the directions are fully understood and potential problems can be avoided. You may find you will want to adapt some projects to simplify procedures or vary the materials required.

4. Many items can be acquired as donations from people or businesses if you plan ahead and make your needs known. Many churches distribute lists of materials needed to their congregation and community and are able to provide crafts at little or no cost. Some items can be brought by the children themselves (e.g., shoe boxes for "Bird House" activity or a cereal box for "Harvest Carts").

5. In making your supplies list, distinguish between items which every individual child will need and those which will be shared among a group.

6. Keep in mind that some materials may be shared among more than one age level, but only if there is good coordination among the groups. It is extremely frustrating to a teacher to expect to have scissors, only to discover another group is using them. Basic supplies which are used repeatedly in craft projects should usually be provided to every group.

List of Materials

Since you will probably never try to do all 101 projects described in this book, we did not attempt to list every item needed. The "Basic Supplies" sections indicate supplies used repeatedly in a large number of the projects for each age level. And the "Specialized Materials" section is intended to call attention to items which are used frequently but might require special effort to secure.

NOTE: A complete list of materials needed for each craft is found in the directions for that specific craft project.

Basic Supplies

For Young Children

Paper—newsprint
      newspaper
      construction
      tissue
      butcher or shelf
Poster board (lightweight cardboard, tagboard, etc.)
Markers—crayons
      felt pens
      pencils
      fine-tip permanent markers
Tape—masking
      transparent
Paint—liquid tempera
Paintbrushes (wide bristle)
Yarn (various colors)
String
Glue—white
      tacky
Scissors—blunt end
Containers—shallow pie tin
      plastic margarine container
Fabric—scraps (solids and prints)
      flannel
      burlap
      felt (variety of colors)
Hole punch
Stapler/Staples
Magazines
Pictures from old Sunday School materials

For Elementary Children

Add to the list for Young Children:
Paint—poster
      acrylic
Paintbrushes (fine tip)
Paper—8½ × 11 white
      tracing
Ball-point pens
Scissors—pointed ends
Chalk/Chalkboard

For Clean Up and Keeping Clean

Smocks (aprons, old shirts, etc.)
Plastic drop cloth
Sponges
Paper towels
Dishpan (if water is not available in room)
Detergent

Specialized Materials

Trim material—ribbon
      lace
      rickrack
      sequins
      glitter
Chenille wire (in a variety of colors)
Clothespins
Craft Sticks
Craft knife
Pom-poms (variety of sizes and colors)
Wrapping paper
Food—lentils
      dry peas
      beans
      popcorn
      elbow & alphabet macaroni

Helpful Hints

Using Glue with Young Children

Since preschoolers have difficulty using glue bottles effectively, you may want to try one of the following procedures. Purchase glue in large containers (up to one gallon size).

a. Pour small amount of glue into several shallow containers.

b. Dilute glue by mixing a little water into each container.

c. Children use paste brushes to spread glue on project.

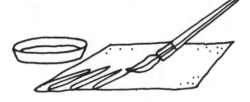

OR

a. Pour a small amount of glue into a plastic margarine tub.

b. Give each child a cotton swab. The child dips the cotton swab into the glue and rubs glue on project.

c. Excess glue can be poured back into the large container at the end of each session.

How to Make Patterns

You will need: Tissue paper, lightweight cardboard, pencil, scissors.

a. Trace pattern from book onto tissue paper.

b. Cut out tissue paper pattern and trace onto cardboard.

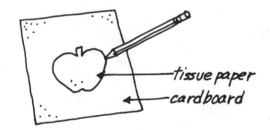

c. Cut out cardboard pattern.

Cutting with Scissors

When cutting with scissors is required for these crafts, take note of the fact that some of the children in your class may be left-handed. It is very difficult for a left-handed person to cut with scissors that were designed to be used with the right hand. Have available in your classroom two or three pairs of left-handed scissors. These can be obtained from a school supply center.

Crafts for Young Children

Craft projects for young children are a blend of "I wanna do it myself!" and "I need help!" Each project, because it is intended to come out looking like a recognizable something, usually requires a certain amount of adult assistance—in preparing a pattern, in doing some cutting, in preselecting magazine pictures, in using the iron, etc.

The younger the child, the more the adult will need to do, but care must always be taken not to rob the child of the satisfaction of his or her own unique efforts. Neither must the adult's desire to have a nice finished project override the child's pleasure at experimenting with color and texture. Avoid the temptation to do the project for the child or to improve on the child's efforts.

Some of the crafts have enrichment and simplification ideas included with them. An enrichment idea provides a way to make the craft more challenging for the older child. A simplification idea helps the younger child complete the craft more successfully. If you find a child frustrated with some of the limitations of working on a structured craft—although most of the projects in this book allow plenty of leeway for children to be themselves—it may be a signal that child needs the opportunity to work on more creative, less structured materials: blank paper and paints, play dough, or abstract collages (gluing miscellaneous shapes or objects onto surfaces such as paper, cardboard or anything else to which glue will adhere). Remember the cardinal rule of thumb in any task a young child undertakes: the process the child goes through is more important than the finished product.

Pop Bottle Terrarium

Materials: Charcoal, potting soil, small bedding plants, glue, scissors, large spoon, decorating materials such as rickrack, lace, felt cut-outs or sequins. For each child—a plastic two-liter pop bottle.

Preparation: Before class, remove the hard plastic base from pop bottle by inserting a large spoon between the bottle and the base and pushing against the base as you rotate the bottle (sketch a). Tip: The base will come off more easily if the bottle is soaked in hot water for a few minutes. Use scissors to cut off the top of the bottle.

Instruct each child in the following procedures:

- Glue decorations to inverted plastic bottle.
- Put a little charcoal in the hard plastic base.
- Fill the base with potting soil, then plant bedding plant.
- Invert the clear plastic bottle over the base, pushing down and turning slightly to tighten (sketch b).

Enrichment Idea: You may want to letter "God loves . . ." and the child's name around the base.

Conversation Suggestions: **God loves us. One way He shows that He loves us is by giving us the things we need. He made the things that plants need, too. What things do plants need to help them grow?** (Soil, light, water.) **God showed how much He loves us by sending His own Son to live with us. Who is God's Son?** (Jesus.)

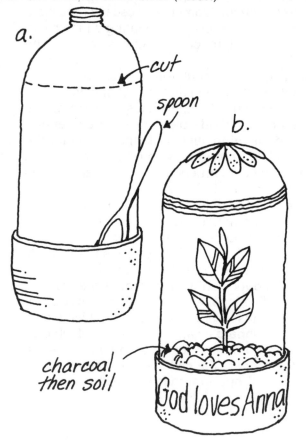

Love Lamb

Materials: Glue, craft sticks, cotton balls, white felt, black chenille wire, scissors, pencils. For each child—white paper plate, medium-sized black pom-pom, two medium wiggle eyes.

Preparation: Using pattern, cut two white felt ears for each lamb. Cut chenille wire into 4-inch (10-cm) lengths.

Instruct each child in the following procedures:

- Cut through the rim of the paper plate at approximately 1-inch (2.5-cm) intervals.
- Using a pencil, curl back the paper plate fringe (sketch a). Younger children may need help with curling the fringe.
- Glue felt ears near edge of plate.
- Use craft stick to spread glue around center of plate. Cover glue with cotton balls.
- Glue on black pom-pom for nose, chenille wire for mouth and wiggle eyes to complete lamb's face.

Conversation Suggestions: **Who made all the animals in the world? Do you have an animal to take care of? How do you show love to your pet? God wants us to show love to animals and especially to each other. How could you show love to your friends? This Love Lamb will help you remember to show love to others.**

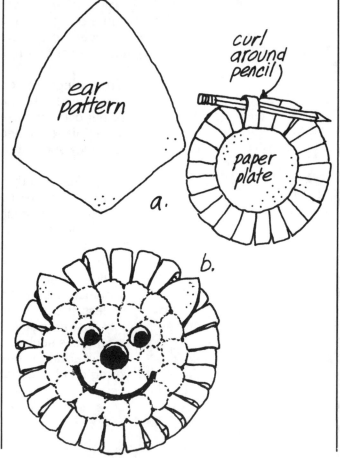

Designer Soap

Materials: Light-colored paper, scissors, fine-tip markers, glue, paraffin wax, loaf pan, water, electric skillet, tongs, newspaper. For each child—new bar of white soap (Ivory).

Preparation: Just prior to project, melt the paraffin in a loaf pan placed inside an electric skillet of boiling water. Be sure to keep these hot items out of children's reach!! Cut paper into rectangles, a little smaller than size of the bar of soap.

Instruct each child in the following procedures:

- Draw a picture or design on piece of paper.
- Glue drawing to bar of soap.

Teacher uses tongs to quickly skim picture side of soap into melted paraffin. Set upright on newspaper and allow to dry. (Paraffin keeps picture from dissolving when soap is used.)

Conversation Suggestions. **Can you think of someone you have had a fight or argument with. How did you feel after the fight? Fighting hurts people. Sometimes bodies get hurt and sometimes feelings get hurt. It is better to be friendly than to fight. How can you be friendly? One friendly thing you can do is give a gift to someone. The soap you made today would be a good gift. Who can you give your soap to?**

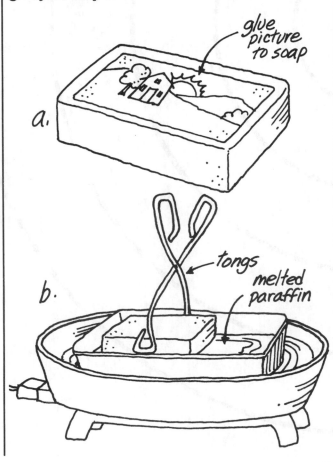

Joy Vine

Materials: Green construction paper, cardboard, glue, green yarn, stapler, staples, dried flowers. Optional—seeds, leaves, flowers or other materials collected on a nature walk.

Preparation: Using a copy machine, reproduce the spiral pattern onto green construction paper—one for each child. Cut yarn into 18-inch (45-cm) lengths—one for each child.

Instruct each child in the following procedures:

- Cut along the spiral lines to make vine. (Younger children may need help in cutting vine.)
- Glue leaves, flowers and other natural decorations to the vine.
- Staple yarn to center end of spiral to form hanger (see sketch).

Conversation Suggestions: **How does it make you feel to go outside on a pretty day? What things do you see that God made? Our Bible says, *(God) . . . made the world and everything in it* (Acts 17:24, NIV). When I see all the beautiful things God made, I feel happiness and joy. You can take your Joy Vine home to help you remember all the special things God made for you to enjoy.**

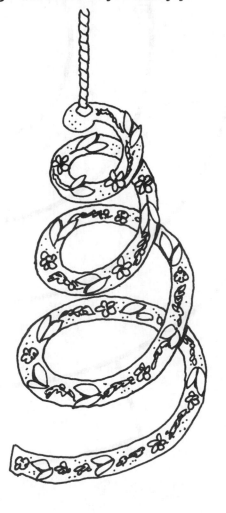

Joy Vine Pattern

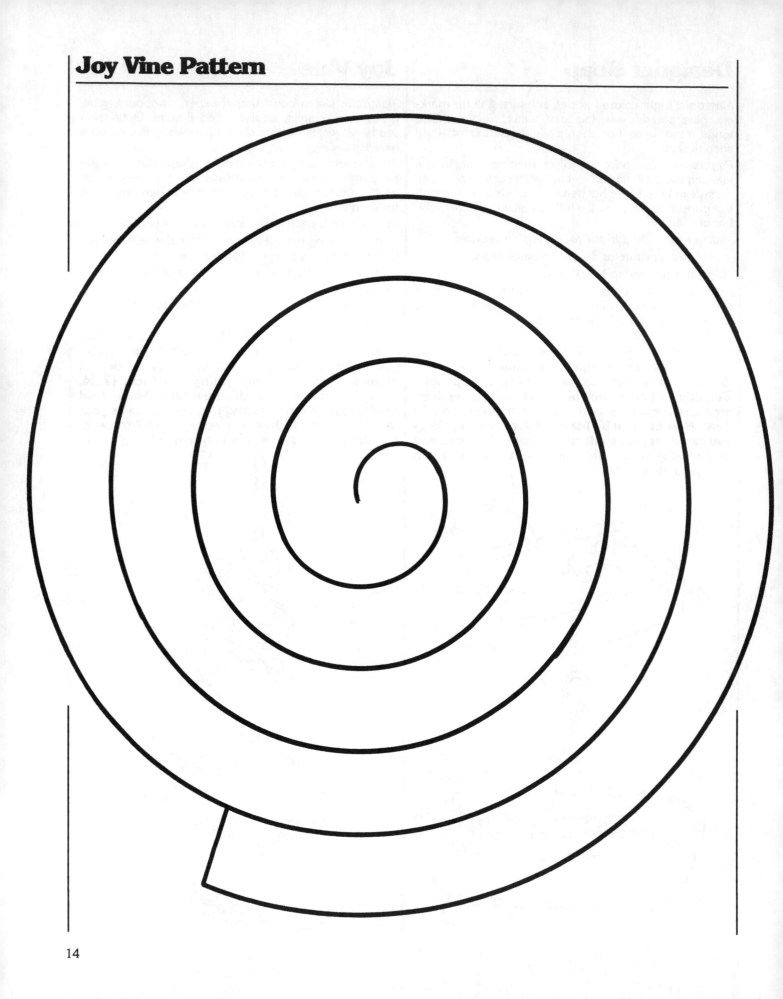

Patience Pal

Materials: Permanent marking pens, glue, potting soil, water in plastic pitcher, large spoons, grass seed. For each child—clear plastic cup, 2 small wiggle eyes, small pom-pom.

Instruct child in the following procedures:

• With marking pen, draw mouth on plastic cup.

• Glue wiggle eyes and pom-pom nose to plastic cup to complete face. Allow a few minutes for glue to dry.

• Carefully spoon potting soil into the cup.

• Scatter a pinch of grass seed on the soil. Water lightly.

Conversation Suggestions: **If you take good care of your Patience Pal, and water it just a little bit, it will grow grass hair in a few days. You will be able to see the grass roots grow down through the soil. That will be fun to see, but it may be hard to wait. A patient person is someone who is good at waiting. When are some times you need to be patient? God wants us all to have patience. When your pal's hair grows long you can give a "haircut" with scissors.**

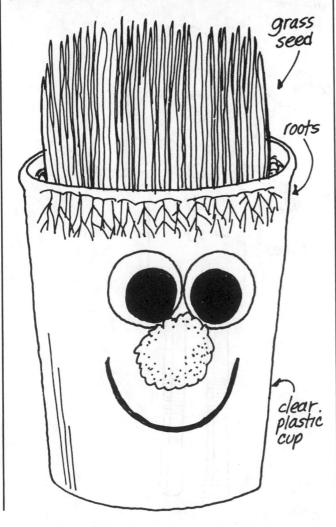

grass seed

roots

clear plastic cup

Color Scope

Materials: White shelf or butcher paper, several colors of tissue paper, small plastic containers, glue, water, paintbrushes, craft knife. For each child—one potato chip can with plastic lid.

Preparation: Use craft knife to cut off bottom end of can. Cut shelf paper to fit around cans. Cover cans with paper. Cut tissue paper into small pieces. Thin glue with small amount of water and pour into small containers.

Instruct each child in the following procedures:

• Brush glue onto covered can. While glue is still wet, decorate can with tissue paper pieces. Set aside to dry (sketch a).

• Using paintbrush, spread glue on inside of plastic lid.

• Place tissue paper on lid, one piece at a time (sketch b).

• Paint over tissue paper with glue.

• Place lid on cut end of can. It will fit loosely so that lid turns.

Simplification Idea: Instead of using tissue paper, decorate cans with felt pens or stickers, or have children use wrapping paper to cover can.

Conversation Suggestions: **Look through your Color Scope. What do you see? God made the light for us to enjoy. He made beautiful colors for us to see. God is good to us. What are some good things you can do?**

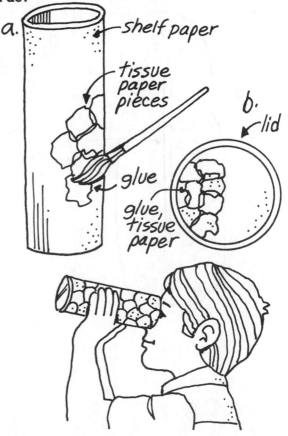

a. shelf paper

tissue paper pieces

b. lid

glue

glue, tissue paper

Clay Helper

Materials: Modeling clay, flexible straws, cotton balls, toothpicks. Optional—unshelled almonds, fine-tip markers, glue, cloves.

Preparation: Divide modeling clay into portions—one handful for each child. For each child—cut the ends off four flexible straws to make four 3-inch (7.5-cm) sections, keeping the flexible joints in the center of each (sketch a).

Instruct each child in the following procedures:

• Divide clay into two pieces—one smaller than the other.

• Mold larger piece of clay into oval shape for body, and smaller piece into round shape for head.

• Using toothpick as "backbone," attach head to body (sketch b). (If using almond for head, make face on almond with felt marker and push into clay body. Rubber cement will help secure almond in place.)

• Insert straw sections into clay body to make arms and legs.

• Place cotton on head for hair. (Cotton will stick to the clay. If using almond, glue the cotton on.)

• Older children may use toothpick to carve facial features onto clay head.

Simplification Idea: Assemble clay figures ahead of time. Let children decorate them.

Enrichment Idea: Push cloves into clay figure for buttons.

Conversation Suggestions: **We made arms and legs on our Clay Helpers. I'm glad God gave us arms and legs, hands and feet. Our Bible says we should show kindness to others. What are some ways we can use our hands and feet to show kindness?**

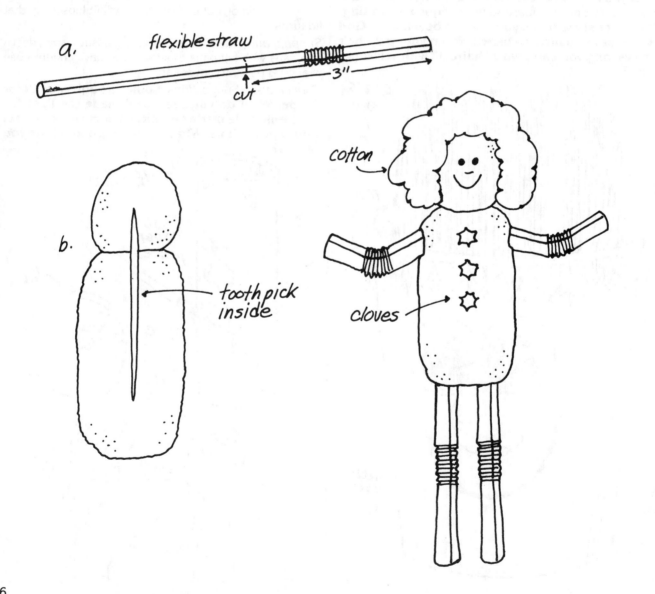

a. flexible straw

cut

3"

b.

toothpick inside

cotton

cloves

Sharing Board

Materials: Poster board or lightweight cardboard, magazines, paper fasteners, marker, scissors, glue. For each child—one plastic margarine lid.

Preparation: Cut poster board into 12-inch (30-cm) squares—one for each child. Write "I can share" along the bottom of each square. Poke hole through center of margarine lid, then through center of poster board. Tear out magazine pages that show pictures of things children can share.

Instruct each child in the following procedures:

- Cut out or tear pictures from magazine pages provided.

- Glue pictures onto poster board (sketch a).

- Use marker to draw a straight line on lid to make pointer (sketch b.).

- Fasten lid to board with paper fastener.

Simplification Idea: Select and pre-cut magazine pictures for each child.

Enrichment Idea: If instant camera is available, take photo of child and glue to margarine lid.

Conversation Suggestions: **Our Bible says to *Do what is right and good* (Deut. 6:18 *NIV*). Remembering to do good things is one way of being faithful. When you share with others, you are doing what is good. What are some things that you can share?** (Have children turn lid to point to objects they can share.) **What is the right thing to do when you have two oranges and another child has none? When you have a toy and another child asks to use it? What are some other ways you can be faithful?** (Tell the truth, do your jobs without having to be reminded, etc.)

a.

I can share

b.

draw line

Flannelgraph

Materials: Black felt squares, flannel or felt fabric scraps, cookie cutters, crayons or paint and paintbrushes, stapler, glue. For each child—10 × 13-inch (25 × 32.5-cm) clasp manila envelope.

Preparation: Hold envelope with clasp at bottom and in back. Fold envelope up 3 inches (7.5 cm) so that clasp and flap are facing front (sketch a). Staple or tape envelope on each side. Cut black felt to fit space above "pocket."

Instruct each child in the following procedures:

• Glue felt square to envelope with bottom edge behind "pocket."

• Decorate pocket with crayons or paint. Cookie cutters can be used as templates.

• Cut flannel into small shapes and place in pocket (sketch b).

Enrichment Idea: Children trace around cookie cutters to make flannel shapes. Letter *Be gentle* on pocket.

Conversation Suggestions: **Can you make a picture on your flannelgraph? Some toys, like this flannelgraph, may tear or break easily. We need to be gentle and careful with some of our toys. How can you be gentle when you make pictures on your flannelgraph? Our Bible says *Be gentle* (Eph. 4:2 *NIV*). What things do we need to be especially gentle with?**

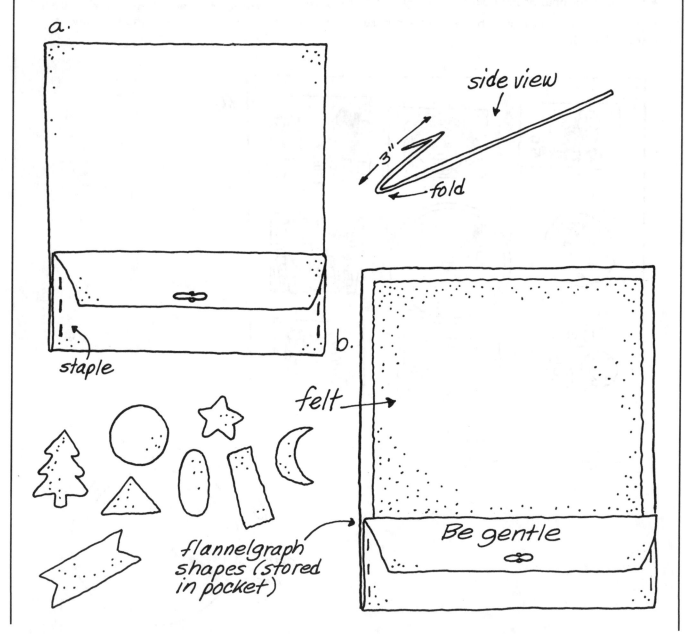

a.

side view

3"

fold

staple

felt

flannelgraph shapes (stored in pocket)

b.

Be gentle

Miniature Puppet Stage

Materials: Felt pens, crayons, stapler and staples, scissors, 8½ × 11-inch (21.5 × 27.5-cm) manila file folders (one for every two children), long-handled wooden ice cream spoons (two for each child).

Preparation: With folded edge at top, cut folder in half to make two narrower folders (sketch a). Cut a 4 × 5-inch (10 × 12.5-cm) window in top flap of each folder (sketch b).

Instruct each child in the following procedures:

• Open folder and use crayons or markers to draw background picture on the half without the window (sketch c).

• Close folder and decorate border with markers or crayons.

• Staple sides of folder together, leaving bottom unstapled (sketch d).

• Draw happy and sad faces on opposite sides of spoons (sketch e).

• Place puppets behind frame of "stage" and act out a scene.

Simplification Idea: Use pre-cut magazine picture for background scenery.

Enrichment Idea: Glue fabric scraps to border of stage for "curtain." Staple a small square of paper to bottom of stage to make a "puppet pocket" to store puppets. Do not let staples close bottom of stage.

Conversation Suggestions: **How does your face look when you are happy? When you are sad? What things make you happy? Sad?** (Encourage children to use puppets to act out happy and sad situations.) **Did your puppets do what THEY wanted to do? No. YOU made them move. You were controlling them. Our Bible says** *Be self-controlled.* (1 Peter 5:8 *NIV*.) **That means you can decide to do what is right. Damon, when you waited patiently for the glue, you were controlling yourself. Lorelei, when you used a quiet voice instead of shouting, you were controlling yourself, too.**

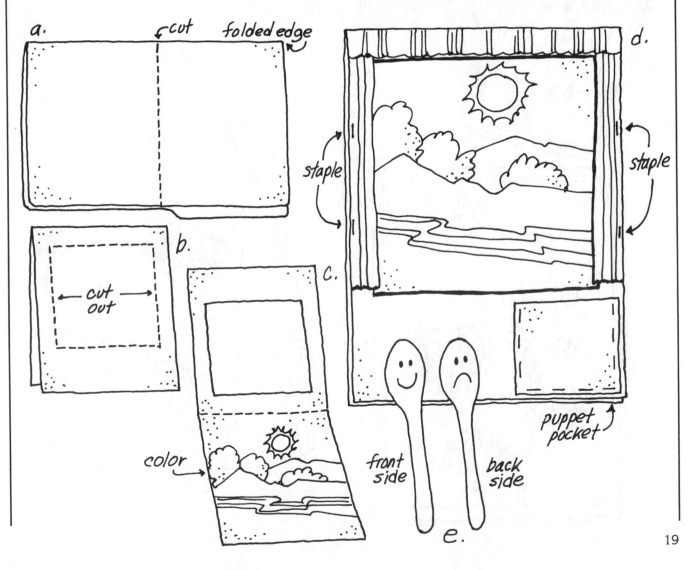

Mosaic

Materials: Pencils, glue, lentils, dried peas, beans, popcorn kernels, chalkboard and chalk or butcher paper and felt markers. For each child—one Styrofoam meat tray.

Preparation: Letter a list of single words (such as love, hope, faith, Jesus) on a chalkboard or sheet of paper. Optional—gather templates or objects for children to trace.

Instruct each child in the following procedures:

• Using a pencil, draw a picture or copy a word onto the meat tray. (Optional—provide templates or objects for children to trace.)

• Draw a line of glue over pencil lines.

• Glue beans onto letters forming the word or simple picture.

Enrichment Idea: Spread glue in the background spaces and fill in with contrasting beans or seeds.

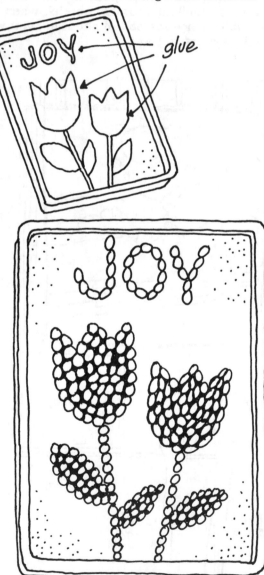

Foam Cuppet

Materials: Scissors, felt pens, scraps of felt or construction paper, feathers, chenille wires, ribbons, yarn, glue. For each child—one Styrofoam cup.

Preparation: Use sharp, pointed scissors to cut two small finger holes at the bottom edge of each cup (see sketch).

Instruct each child in the following procedures:

• Use felt pens to draw a person, animal or object on the cup.

• Cut facial features or other decorations from paper or felt and glue in place.

• Push chenille wires and feathers into cup to make hair.

Enrichment Idea: Have child practice walking the puppet on a table top. Child may use puppet to help tell one thing learned in class today. You might want to have each child make two puppets, so the puppets can talk to each other.

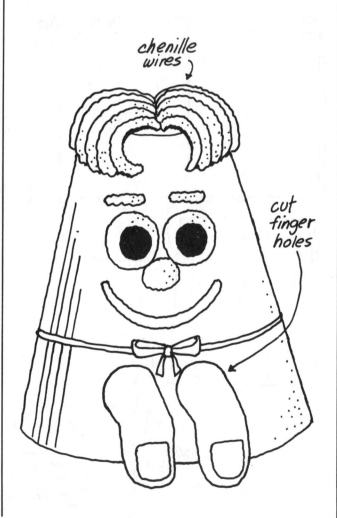

Egg Cup Lei

Materials: Hole punch, masking tape, yarn, scissors. For each child—one colored Styrofoam egg carton (having a variety of colors of cartons will make leis more colorful and appealing). Optional—plastic bags.

Preparation: Cut yarn into 24-inch (60-cm) lengths. Cut the tops off egg cartons. Cut out the twelve separate egg cups (sketch a). Using the point of the scissors, cut a small hole in the bottom of each egg cup (or use a sharp pencil to poke holes). From the lid, cut twelve 2-inch (5-cm) squares or other shapes. Wrap a small piece of tape around one end of each length of yarn. Optional—place cups and squares for each child in separate plastic bag.

Instruct each child in the following procedures:

• Using a hole punch, punch a hole in the center of each square.

• Thread yarn through an egg cup and then a square (sketch b). Repeat process using all the egg cups and squares.

• Tie the two ends of the yarn together (sketch c).

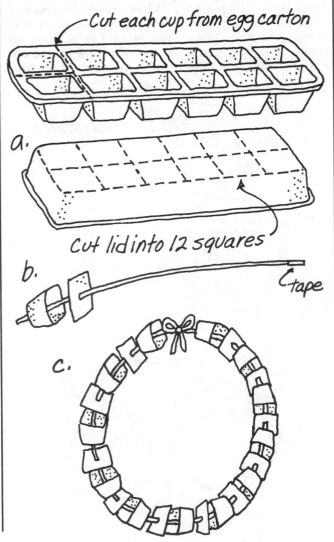

Cut each cup from egg carton

a.

Cut lid into 12 squares

b. tape

c.

Paper Shaker

Materials: Dried beans, yarn, felt pens, stapler, hole punch. For each child—one paper plate.

Preparation: Cut yarn into 6-inch (15-cm) lengths.

Instruct each child in the following procedures:

• Decorate the bottom side of plate with felt pens. Fold the plate in half, decorated side out.

• Staple three-fourths of the way around the folded edge, as in sketch a. (Assist the children.)

• Drop a small handful of beans in the opening (sketch a).

• Staple the opening.

• Punch three or four holes around the edge of the plate.

• Insert a piece of yarn in each hole.

• Tie yarn so both ends hang free (sketch b).

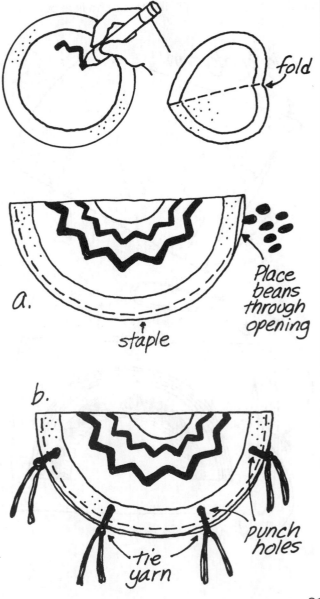

fold

a. staple

Place beans through opening

b.

tie yarn

punch holes

Wind Bagger

Materials: Hole punch, string, tempera paint and paintbrushes, crayons or felt pens. For each child—one large, flat, light-weight paper bag.

Preparation: Cut string into 6- to 8-foot lengths (1.8- to 2.4-m)—one for each child. Fold in the open edge of each bag about one inch to reinforce the opening (sketch a).

Instruct each child in the following procedures:
- Decorate the bag with paint, crayons or felt pens.
- Punch a hole through bag on one side of folded edge. (Optional—punch hole in both sides and tie a string in each hole.)
- Insert the string and tie it in a knot (sketch b).

Enrichment Idea: Help the children make a loop in the end of the string for ease in holding. NOTE: Instruct children to hold the string of their bags and run into the wind. The open end will fill with air and flare out.

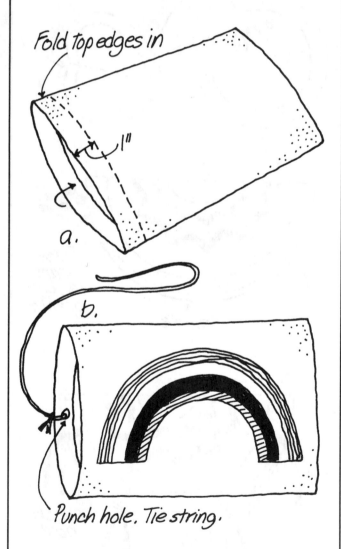

Fold top edges in

1"

a.

b.

Punch hole. Tie string.

Grace Mat

Materials: Liquid starch, large paintbrushes, margarine tubs, waxed paper, scissors, magazines, paper, felt pens.

Preparation: Pour liquid starch into margarine containers. Cut waxed paper into 9 × 12-inch (22.5 × 30-cm) sheets—two for each child.

Instruct each child in the following procedures:
- Cut or tear pictures of food from magazines.
- Write a short table grace on piece of paper. (E.g., Thank you, God, for my food.)
- Cover one sheet of waxed paper with starch using paintbrush.
- Arrange the food cutouts and "grace" paper on top of the starch.
- Lightly brush another coat of starch over the entire mat.
- Place the second sheet of waxed paper on top of the mat.
- Allow mat to dry, then assist children in trimming the uneven edges with scissors.

Conversation Suggestions: **What prayer do you say at home before you eat?** (Volunteers may share their family's mealtime prayer with group.) **It is good to thank God for the food we eat. Your grace mat will remind you to tell God thank you each time you eat.**

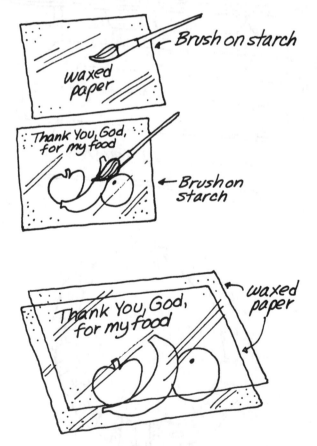

Brush on starch

waxed paper

Thank You, God, for my food

Brush on starch

Thank You, God, for my food

waxed paper

Worm Fingerling

Materials: Green felt, black construction paper, glue, hole punch. For each child—four small green pom-poms.

Preparation: Trace pattern onto green felt twice for each child and cut out.

Instruct each child in the following procedures:

• Draw a line of glue around the rounded edge of one green felt piece (not on straight edge) as in sketch a.

• Place the second piece on top and press tightly.

• Assist children in punching two black circles from construction paper and glue in place for eyes (sketch b).

• Glue four pom-poms across the top to form the worm's back. Let worm dry.

Instruct child to slip a finger in the open end of worm. Child can use the fingerling as a regular finger puppet or as a bookworm who helps him or her turn the pages.

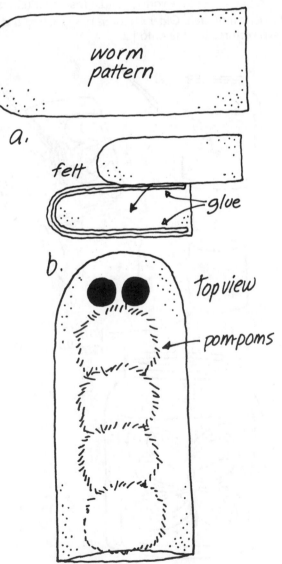

Clothespin Note Holder

Materials: Glue, heavy poster board, alphabet and elbow macaroni, green felt-tip marker. For each child—one clip-type clothespin.

Preparation: From poster board, cut a 2½-inch (6.25-cm) square for each child.

Instruct each child in the following procedures:

• Glue the macaroni onto the square, spelling out his or her name. (If alphabet macaroni is hard to find, have children form flowers with the elbow macaroni. Draw stems and leaves with the green marker.)

• Glue macaroni around edge of square to make border (sketch a).

• When macaroni is partially set, glue the handle of the clothespin to the back of cardboard. (Make sure the bottom of the square meets the end of the clothespin so it will stand by itself.)

Rainbow Bookmark

Materials: Grosgrain rainbow ribbon, white felt, scissors, glue. Optional—paper, felt pen, sequins or glitter.

Preparation: Use pattern to cut two identical felt clouds for each child. Cut ribbon into 6-inch (15-cm) lengths—one for each child.

Instruct each child in the following procedures:

• Glue one felt cloud to the end of a length of ribbon.

• Draw a line of glue around edge of cloud and place other cloud on top, matching edges.

Enrichment Idea: Print a Bible verse on a small piece of paper, one for each child. Glue Bible verse paper to the cloud. Glue glitter or sequins around Bible verse.

Candle Holder

Materials: Glue, paintbrushes, small containers (plastic margarine tubs, etc.), clear glitter (sometimes called "Diamond Dust"), small pictures from old Sunday School materials, wrapping paper or greeting cards. For each child—a small, clean baby food jar. Optional—a votive candle for each child, scissors.

Preparation: Choose pictures that are blank on the reverse side and cut pictures to fit the side of a baby food jar. (Older children may be able to select and cut the pictures themselves.) Thin glue slightly with water and pour into containers.

Instruct each child in the following procedures:

• Use paintbrush to glue picture to side of baby food jar (sketch a).

• Hold jar upside down on two extended fingers and paint entire surface with glue (sketch b).

• Sprinkle clear glitter all over wet jar. Let dry.

Optional—place votive candle inside jar (sketch c).

Enrichment Idea: Older children may wish to draw their own pictures to glue onto jar.

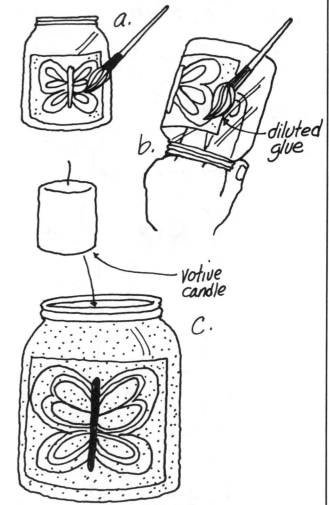

Clothespin Butterfly

Materials: Multi-colored tissue paper, scissors, fine-tip felt pens. For each child—round-end wooden clothespin, one chenille wire.

Preparation: Cut tissue paper into 8-inch (20-cm) squares—two for each child. Cut chenille wire into 6-inch (15-cm) lengths.

Instruct each child in the following procedures:

- Lay one square of tissue paper on top of the other.

- Accordion pleat the squares using small folds (sketch a). Youngest children may gather the paper instead of pleating.

- Keeping the folds together, slide the flattened center of the tissue through the slit in the clothespin (sketch b).

- Fan out the folds to form the wings.

- Twist the chenille wire around head of clothespin for the antenna (sketch c).

- Draw facial features on top of clothespin.

Conversation Suggestions: **Have you ever seen a real butterfly? What color was it? What did you see it do? Could we make a real butterfly? Why not? Our Bible says,** *God made everything.* **(See Ecclesiastes 3:11.) What other things has God made for us to enjoy?**

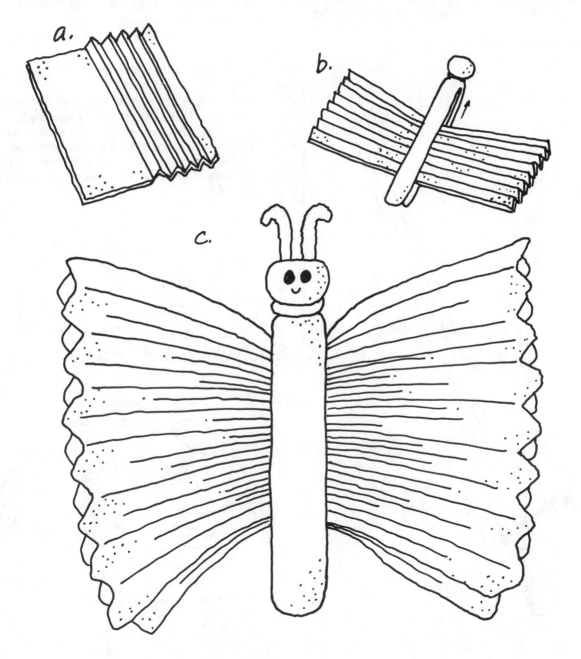

Caterpillar Pencil

Materials: Glue, paper, narrow ribbon. For each child—new unsharpened pencil, four ½-inch (1.25-cm) green pom-poms, two small wiggle eyes.

Preparation: Cut ribbon into 4-inch (10-cm) lengths—one for each child.

Instruct each child in the following procedures:

- Glue pom-poms in a straight line near eraser end of pencil. Let dry.
- Glue eyes to the last pom-pom facing the eraser (see sketch).
- Tie ribbon around the caterpillar's neck.

Conversation Suggestions: **Let's name things God has made that crawl on the ground** (caterpillars, bugs, snakes). **That fly in the sky. That swim in the water. That run on the land. That climb trees. God has made so many kinds of living things!**

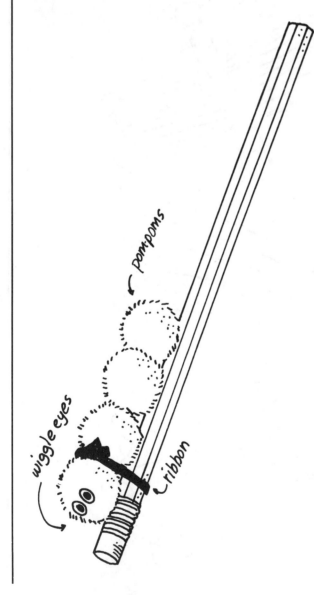

Paperweight

Materials: Cornstarch, baking soda, measuring cup, water, food coloring, spoon, saucepan, stove or hot plate, buttons, marbles, pebbles or small shells, airtight container for dough, dampened paper towels for cleanup.

Preparation: Make dough by combining food coloring with 1¼ cups water, then add to 1 cup cornstarch and 2 cups baking soda in a saucepan. Cook over medium heat, stirring constantly until dough-like and stiff. Store in airtight container until ready to use. If dough crumbles when ready to use, moisten hands and knead. Recipe makes enough dough for approximately six 3-inch (7.5-cm) balls.

Instruct each child in the following procedures:

- Roll handful of dough into a ball.
- Press dough onto table to form a flat bottom.
- Decorate paperweight with buttons, marbles, pebbles or small shells by pressing them firmly into dough ball. Let dry.

Conversation Suggestions: Demonstrate the use of a completed paperweight. **I think your paperweight will make a nice gift for you to give to someone you love. Think of a person you want to give your gift to.** Allow children to respond. **Giving gifts is a way we show our love. God tells us to *Love one another.*** (See 1 John 4:7.)

Roll dough into a ball   Flatten bottom

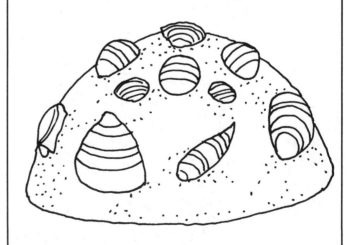

Refrigerator Magnet

Materials: Magnetic tape, red felt, small decorative materials (e.g., rickrack, yarn, dried lima beans), glue, lightweight cardboard, scissors. For each child—metal lid from pull-top frozen juice container.

Preparation: Cut magnetic strip into 1½-inch (3.75-cm) pieces—one for each child. Use pattern to make red felt hearts—one for each child.

Instruct each child in the following procedures:

• Glue magnetic strip to bottom of lid.

• Glue heart to top of lid (side with edges turned up).

• Put a line of glue around outside edge of heart.

• Arrange decorative material on the glue (see sketch). Let dry.

Conversation Suggestions: **When you see a heart, what do you think of? A heart reminds us of love. Who is someone you love? And your (mother) loves you very much! I'm thinking of someone who loves you even more than your (mother). Can you think who that someone is? God loves you with the very best kind of love, for *God is love.*** (See 1 John 4:8.)

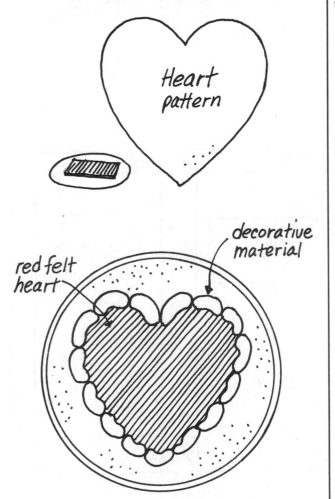

Craft Stick Trivet

Materials: Wide tip felt markers in a variety of colors, glue, newsprint or butcher paper, damp paper towels for cleanup. For each child—thirteen Popsicle or craft sticks.

Preparation: Cover work area with newsprint. At each child's place, draw two large black dots, 3 inches (7.5 cm) apart.

Instruct each child in the following procedures:

• Color sticks with felt pens.

• Place two sticks, parallel to each other, 3 inches (7.5 cm) apart. (Use guideline dots as in sketch a.)

• Run a line of glue on top of each stick (sketch a).

• Place remaining sticks side by side across the glued sticks (sketch b). Let dry.

Conversation Suggestions: **What colors are you making your sticks? Shut your eyes. Touch the sticks you have colored. Can you tell which one is (red) by touching it? Why not? What has God made to help you know which stick is (red)? Your eyes are a wonderful gift from God. Let's thank Him for making your wonderful eyes.** Pray a brief prayer of thanks to God.

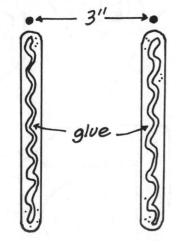

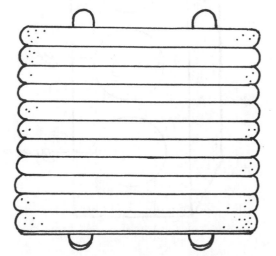

Traffic Signs

Materials: Black, white, red, yellow and green construction paper, scissors, glue, water, shallow containers, paste brushes, rubber bands, felt markers. For each child—empty quart milk carton.

Preparation: Cut top off each milk carton. Rinse and dry. Cut black paper to fit sides of carton—four rectangles for each child. Cut 2-inch (5-cm) circles from red, yellow and green construction paper—one set for each child. Mix glue with water until mixture spreads easily with brush. Pour into containers. Optional—cut and letter a stop sign and a yield sign—one set for each child (sketch a).

Instruct each child in the following procedures:

- Glue black rectangles on milk carton to cover.
- Hold paper in place with rubber bands and let dry.
- Glue red, then yellow, then green circles down one side of the carton (sketch b).

Enrichment Idea: On other sides of carton glue "stop" and "yield" signs (sketch b).

Conversation Suggestions: As children complete traffic signs, ask, **When the red circle is lighted, what are you to do? Does the lighted red circle mean to stop if you want to? We must stop every time we see it lighted.** Continue similarly with yellow and green circles. **Brian, show us your "stop" sign. Have you ever seen this sign? Where? What did your** (dad) **do? Dana, show us your "yield" sign.** Be sure children understand "yield" means "let others go before you go." **Why is obeying traffic signs an important thing to do? What has God given you to help you obey traffic signs?** (Eyes to see, ears to hear, a mind to think.)

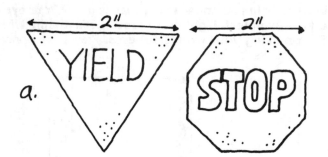

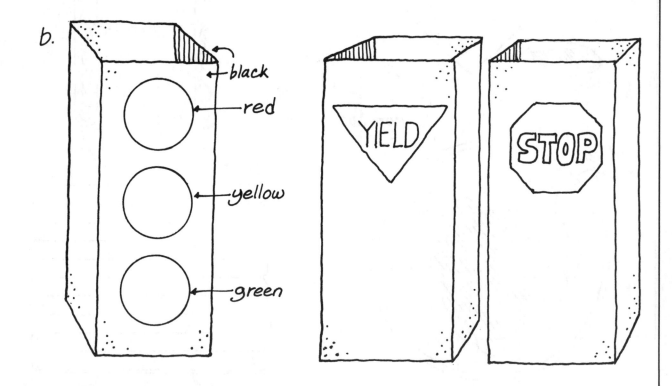

Bottle Vase

Materials: Brightly colored (not pastel) tissue paper, glue, paste brushes, water, shallow containers. For each child—empty, glass bottle with smooth round sides (catsup bottle works well).

Preparation: Cut the tissue paper into assorted shapes and sizes. Mix equal amounts of glue and water in the containers.

Instruct each child in the following procedures:

• Brush glue mixture onto a section of the bottle.

• Place tissue piece on the bottle and smooth out with brush.

• Continue the process, overlapping the tissue, until bottle is covered.

• Brush on a top coat of glue and let dry.

Conversation Suggestions: **What colors are you using on your vase? What is your favorite color? Name some things that are** (purple). **Did you know dogs cannot see color? Aren't you glad God made your eyes so you can enjoy seeing all the colors in our beautiful world!**

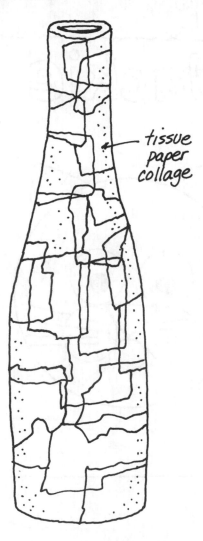

tissue paper collage

Burlap Place Mat

Materials: Felt scraps in a variety of colors, glue, paste brushes, shallow containers, water, measuring stick, felt pen, tan burlap, scissors.

Preparation: Cut burlap into 9x12-inch (22.5 × 30-cm) pieces—one for each child. Use measuring stick and felt pen to clearly mark a line 1 inch (2.5 cm) from each edge of burlap (sketch a). Thin glue with water until mixture spreads easily with brush. Pour into containers. Cut felt into 2-inch (5-cm) circles, triangles and squares.

Instruct each child in the following procedures:

• Unravel each side of burlap to the "stop" line. (Demonstrate how to unravel threads of burlap.)

• Experiment arranging felt shapes into a design.

• Glue felt shapes to burlap (sketch b).

Conversation Suggestions: As children work, ask simple questions to increase awareness of God's gifts. **What has God given you so you can make your place mat?** (Eyes, to see, hands to work, a mind to think, ears to listen to teacher and friends.) **When we think about what God has given us, we need to do something very important. What could it be?** (Thank Him.) **Our Bible says,** *Give thanks to the Lord, for he is good* (Psalm 136:1, *NIV*). Pray a brief prayer of thanks to God for His gifts. Ask volunteers to pray with you. **Nickie, which gift would you like to thank God for? Then you may say, 'Thank You, God for our eyes.'**

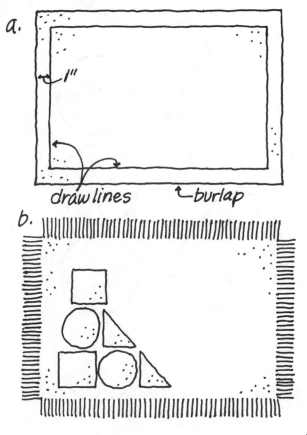

a.

1"

draw lines   burlap

b.

Kitty Bag

Materials: Construction paper, crayons, glue, water, paste brushes, shallow containers. For each child—medium-sized paper bag (bottom measurement approximately 6 × 8½ inches (15 × 21.5 cm).

Preparation: Thin glue with water until mixture spreads easily with paste brush. Pour into containers. From construction paper, cut three triangles and six circles, using the dimensions shown in sketch a—one set for each child. Make a sample bag following the directions below.

Instruct each child in the following procedures:

- Glue circles and triangles on side of bag to form cat's face (sketch b).
- Add whiskers with crayon.
- Letter name across top of bag.

Conversation Suggestions: Child may place items in bag each day, then take bag home the last day of the school. **When it's time to put away your toys, where do you put your little trucks? Your small building blocks? You can help by putting them in your Kitty Bag. Then you'll know just where they are the next time you want them. Helping put away your toys is a good thing to do. What other ways do you help at your house? Helping is a way to show we *love one another*** (see 1 John 4:7).

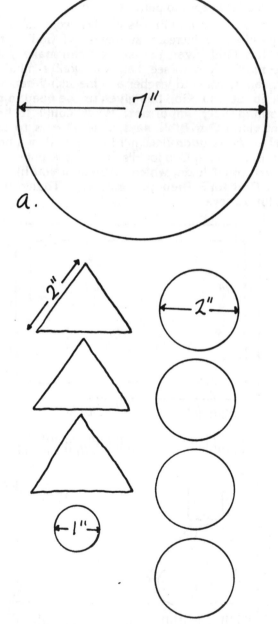

Crafts for Younger Elementary

Children in the first few years of school are delights to work with in completing craft projects. They have a handle on most of the basic skills needed, they are eager to do things and their taste in art has usually not yet surpassed their ability to produce. In other words, they generally like the things they make.

Since reading ability is not a factor in most craft projects, crafts can be a great leveler among a group.

Some children excel here who may or may not be top achievers in other areas.

Many of the projects in this session also appeal to preschoolers, and as long as an adult works closely with them, they can succeed. Older children will enjoy some of these also, enjoying the fairly simple procedures required.

Good Choice Apple

Materials: Red and green felt, white paper, lightweight cardboard, felt-tip pens, sharp scissors, glue, medium-sized beads.

Preparation: Using lightweight cardboard, make apple and leaf patterns—one for every two or three children. Cut remaining cardboard into 1 × 6-inch (2.5 × 15-cm) strips—one for each child. Cut paper into 3-inch (7.5-cm) squares—one for each child.

Instruct each child in the following procedures:

• Trace Apple Pattern onto red felt, then onto cardboard. Cut out both.

• Trace leaf pattern onto green felt. Cut out.

• Cut a door into the middle of felt apple (sketch a).

• Letter "God says" on the door with felt tip pen.

• To make knob, glue bead onto the right edge of the door.

• Glue paper square onto center of cardboard apple (sketch b).

• Glue felt apple to cardboard apple. (Do NOT glue the door. The door opens to reveal lettering behind it.)

• Letter "Make good choices" on paper square.

• Glue the leaf behind the stem.

• Fold cardboard strip in half for stand.

• Glue stand to back of apple (sketch c).

Simplification Idea: Pre-cut apples and leaves from felt.

Conversation Suggestions: **Adam and Eve chose to eat the fruit God had told them not to eat.** (It was probably not an apple, but some other kind of fruit.) **Did they make a good choice? They disobeyed God, but He still loved them. God loves you, too. He wants you to choose to obey Him. In what ways can you obey God? What good choices can you make?**

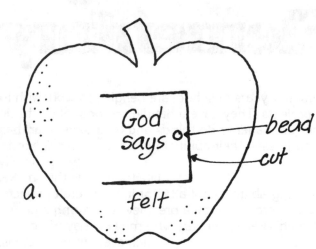

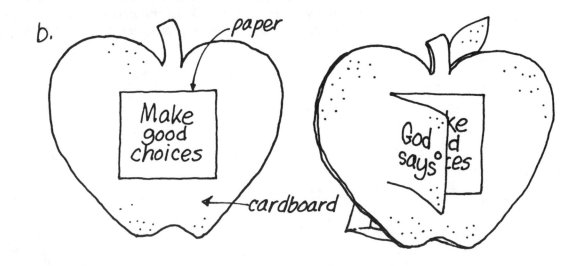

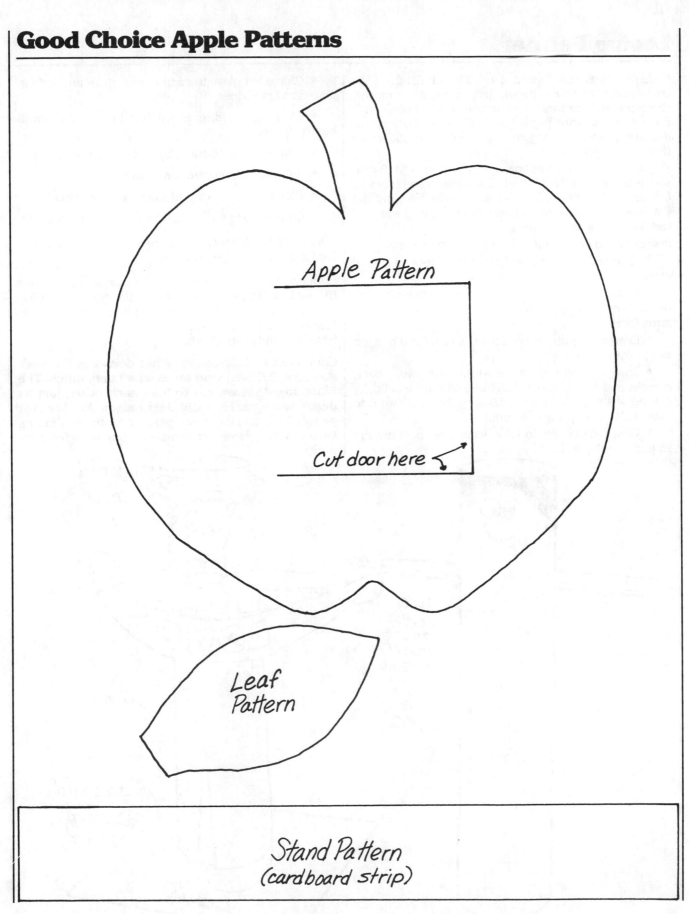

Apple Pattern

Cut door here

Leaf
Pattern

Stand Pattern
(cardboard strip)

Loving Farmer

Materials: Heavy cardboard, 8½ × 11-inch (21.5 × 27.5-cm) sheets of white paper, felt, tagboard, crayons, sharp-pointed scissors, glue, pencils or ball-point pens. For each child—one paper towel tube, one plastic drinking straw, two small wiggle eyes, a small plastic jar lid (from spice jar).

Preparation: Cut cardboard into 4-inch (10-cm) squares—one for each child. Cut paper towel tubes to 8½ inches (21.5-cm). Cut Glove, Overalls, Feet and Hat Patterns from tagboard. Optional—pre-cut gloves and feet for less mature learners.

Instruct each child in the following procedures:

• Cover tube with a sheet of white paper and glue in place.

• Using pencil or ball-point pen, poke holes in tube 6½ inches (16.25- cm) from bottom and insert straw for arms (sketch a.)

• Draw a face above the farmer's arms and glue on wiggle eyes (sketch a).

• Trace patterns onto felt—one hat, two gloves, overalls and feet. Cut out. (Children who have difficulty cutting will need help with this step. You may want to have the smaller pieces pre-cut.)

• Glue felt overalls to tube, wrapping them around so ends overlap in back.

• Glue a felt glove to each end of straw and hold in place until glue dries.

• To make stand, glue felt feet to center of cardboard square.

• Attach farmer to stand by gluing tube on the feet.

• Write "Love" on cardboard stand.

• Glue felt circle to top of tube for base of hat.

• Glue jar lid to felt circle to complete hat (sketch b).

Simplification Idea: Use construction paper instead of felt for overalls, gloves, etc.

Enrichment Idea: Have each student cut a strip of paper 8½-inches (21.5-cm) long, then letter the word LOVE across the paper. (You may also want to include a Bible Memory Verse reference.) Glue ends of banner to farmer's hands (sketch b).

Conversation Suggestions: **What does the Farmer's stand say?** (Love.) **God loves us all very much. The Bible says that we are to love each other, just as Jesus loves us. How did Jesus show His love for people?** (By helping them, praying for them, showing kindness, etc.) **How can we show our love for people?**

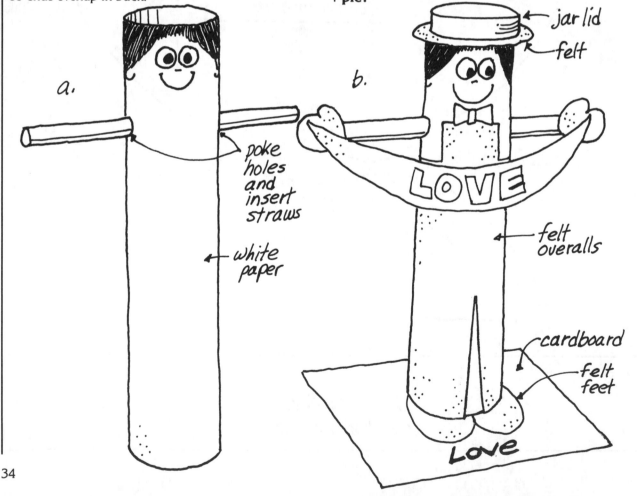

a.
poke holes and insert straws
white paper

b.
jar lid
felt
LOVE
felt overalls
cardboard
felt feet
Love

Loving Farmer Patterns

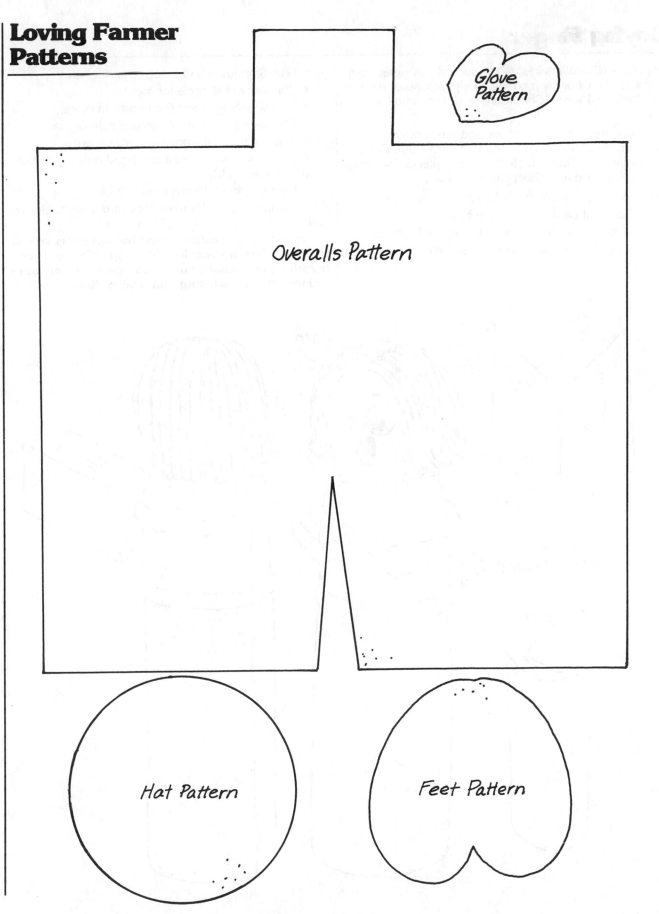

Glove Pattern

Overalls Pattern

Hat Pattern

Feet Pattern

Joyful Singer

Materials: Chenille wires, felt, tagboard, felt pens, yarn, scissors, glue. For each child—one plastic spice jar, one 1½-inch (3.75-cm) Styrofoam ball, two small wiggle eyes.

Preparation: Cut felt to fit around jars, approximately 4 × 6-inches (10 × 15-cm)—one for each child. Cut tagboard into 2 × 2½-inch (5 × 6.25-cm) pieces for songbooks. Cut yarn into short pieces for hair.

Instruct each child in the following procedures:
- Fold tagboard songbook in half.
- Write the word "Joy" inside songbook (sketch a).
- Wrap felt around plastic jar and glue overlapping ends together.
- Secure felt at waist with chenille wire.
- Glue Styrofoam ball to top of jar for head.
- Cut a small felt circle for mouth.
- Glue wiggle eyes and felt mouth in place.
- Glue yarn pieces on Styrofoam ball for hair.
- Wrap chenille wire around body for arms.
- Secure wire with a twist and bend arms up to hold songbook (sketch b).
- Glue songbook to arms (sketch c).

Simplification Idea: Prepare tagboard songbooks by folding and lettering ahead of time.

Conversation Suggestions: **God has given us voices to sing. When do you like to sing? What are your favorite songs about God? God gave us very special voices that can sing and praise Him.**

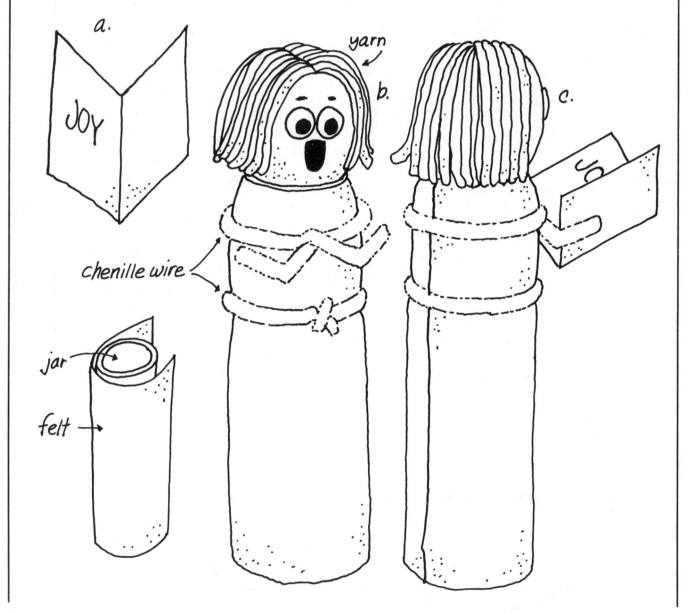

Peace Wall Hanging

Materials: Fine-tipped felt pens, glue, scissors, hole punch, yarn, dried flowers, very small pinecones or leaves, chalk and chalkboard (or butcher paper). For each child—round plastic lid (from large margarine or whipped topping tub), 5-inch (12.5-cm) paper doily.

Preparation: Letter "Peace with God gives friendship with others" on chalkboard. Cut yarn into 8-inch (20-cm) lengths—one for each child.

Instruct each child in the following procedures:

• Letter "Peace with God gives friendship with others" in the center of the doily.

• Punch two holes near top of lid.

• Thread yarn through the holes and tie ends to secure (sketch a).

• Glue doily to inside of lid.

• Glue flowers, pinecones, leaves, etc. around the edges of the doily (sketch b).

Conversation Suggestions: **What does it mean to have peace with God? How does having peace with God help you to be friends with others? How can you show God's peace to your friends?**

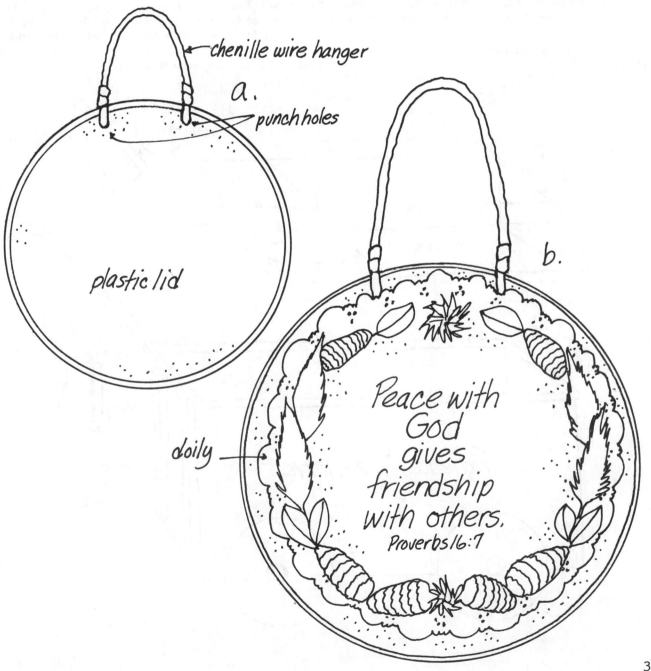

chenille wire hanger

a.

punch holes

plastic lid

doily

Peace with God gives friendship with others. Proverbs 16:7

b.

37

"Patience . . . Then Harvest" Cart

Materials: Cardboard, shelf or butcher paper, felt-tip pens, glue, sharp-pointed scissors, crayons. For each child—one small cereal, cake mix or cracker box, one chenille wire, four metal paper fasteners.

Preparation: Cut 1½-inch (3.75-cm) circles from cardboard—four for each child. Cut each box to a 2½-inch (6.25-cm) height. Set box on shelf paper and measure out the height of box in all four directions. Cut shelf paper as shown in sketch a—one for each child.

Instruct each child in the following procedures:

• Glue pre-cut paper to box to cover all sides.

• Color four cardboard circles for wheels. Use scissors to poke hole in center of each wheel. Put fastener through hole, poke through box then spread ends to secure (sketch b).

• Bend and glue chenille wire to end of box for handle (sketch c).

• Letter "Patience . . . Then Harvest" on the side of the cart.

Simplification Idea: Spray paint the boxes ahead of time instead of covering them with paper.

Enrichment Idea: Children may decorate cart with crayon drawings, then glue chenille wire around top edge of box.

Conversation Suggestions: **This little cart can hold many things. What would you like to put in your cart after you take it home?** (Crayons, pencils, erasers, unused teabags, note paper, etc.) **What does the word harvest mean? What does a farmer use a cart for?** (To carry the food he has just harvested.) **The farmer needs to be patient while his plants are growing. He waits patiently then, when the food is ripe, enjoys the harvest. This little cart is a reminder that we must have patience, too.**

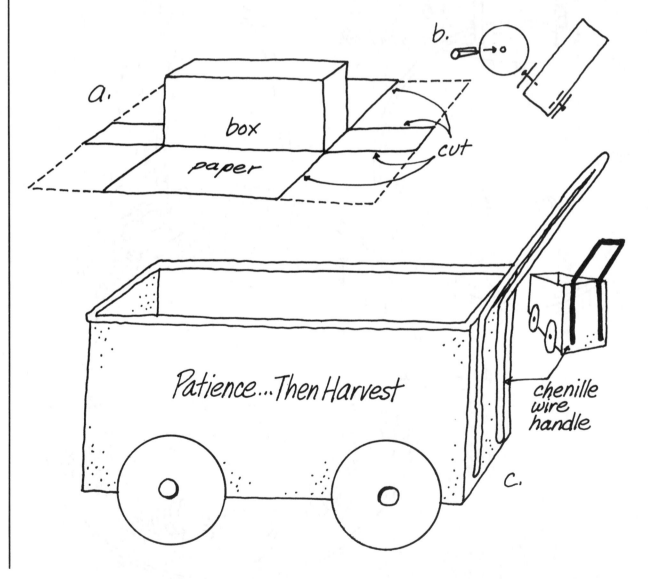

Note Box

Materials: Scissors, pens, sheets of writing paper in various colors, paper cutter, rulers. For each child—one empty square "designer" tissue box.

Preparation: Use paper cutter to cut writing paper into 4½-inch (11.25-cm) squares—at least twenty for each child.

Instruct each child in the following procedures:

• Cut top off tissue box, so that box is 3-inches (7.5-cm) high (sketch a). NOTE: Teacher should start the cutting with sharp-pointed scissors and allow child to complete cutting with regular scissors.

• Measure and cut 2-inch wide (5-cm) opening in one side of box (sketch b).

• Choose twenty squares of writing paper. Place papers in box, creating a pattern with the varied colors.

• Write a nice note to someone on one paper and place it on the top of the stack, or exchange notes with friends in the class.

Enrichment Idea: Letter "Be kind to one another" on side of box.

Conversation Suggestions: **Do you enjoy writing notes? Who would you like to write a note to? What can you say in your note? You can keep your note box to remind you to write kind notes to people, or you can give it to someone as a gift.**

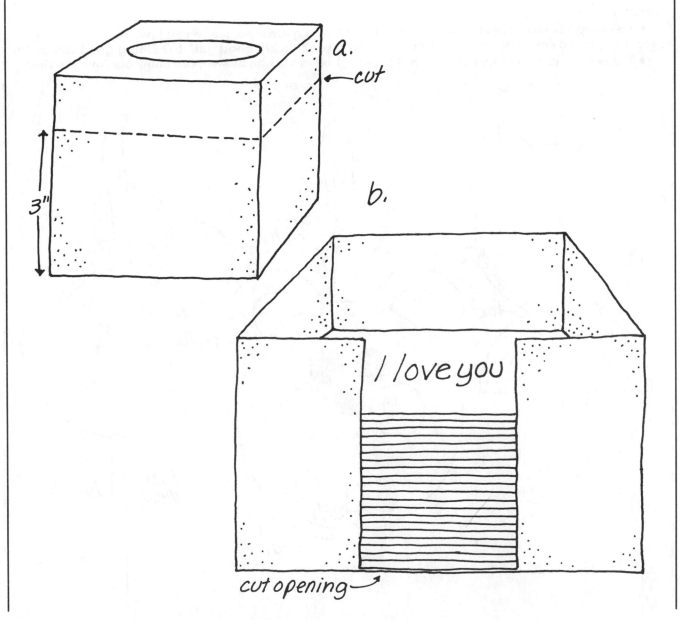

a.
← cut

3"

b.

I love you

cut opening →

"Beary" Good Gift

Materials: Construction paper (brown, black, red, yellow, green), tagboard, scissors, glue, hole punch, narrow ribbon, felt-tip pens. For each child—one lollipop.

Preparation: Using tagboard, make several Bear Patterns. Trace Cheek and Ear Pattern onto yellow and red construction paper and cut out—three circles for each child. (Children may choose from red and yellow circles.) Cut ribbon into 5-inch (12.5-cm) lengths—two for each child.

Instruct each child in the following procedures:

• Trace bear pattern onto brown construction paper. Cut out.

• Place a small stream of glue along the glue lines (sketch a).

• Fold bear at the fold line and press to set glue (sketch a).

• Make paper hole punches from black construction paper for eyes and nose. Glue on bear's face.

• Cut one construction paper circle in half for ears. Glue one half to each ear (sketch b).

• Glue remaining two paper circles in place for cheeks.

• Tie a bow with one of the ribbons. Glue to bear's neck.

• Glue other ribbon together to form loop. Glue to back side of bear.

• Cut a small inverted V under bear's bowtie and insert lollipop through slit (sketch c).

Simplification Idea: Pre-cut bears for children or photocopy pattern onto brown construction paper for children to cut out. Tie ribbons into small bows for bears' bowties.

Enrichment Idea: Letter Bible Memory Verse on back of bear.

Conversation Suggestions: **Your bear would make a nice gift for someone you love. Who can you give your "beary good gift" to? Doing good things for others is one way we can show our love for God.**

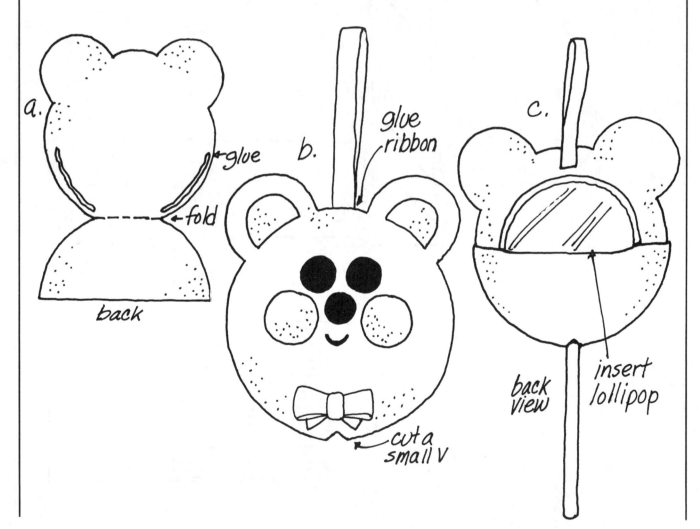

a. →glue ←fold back

b. glue ribbon cut a small V

c. back view insert lollipop

"Beary" Good Gift Pattern

Bear
Pattern

Cheek
and
Ear →
Pattern

Faithful Helper Basket

Materials: Aluminum foil, seam binding, cording or ribbon, glue, white paper, crayons, scissors, hole punch. For each child—lid to sturdy gift box, about 10 × 13-inches (25 × 32.5-cm).

Preparation: Cut ribbon into 24-inch (60-cm) lengths—two for each child. Cut a 5-inch (12.5-cm) length of ribbon for each child. Cut foil into 11 × 14-inch (27.5 × 35-cm) pieces—one for each child. Cut paper into strips to fit sides of boxes—four strips per child.

Instruct each child in the following procedures:

• Line bottom of box with foil and glue in place. (This will waterproof the bottom of the box.)

• Use crayons to color flowers, vegetables and fruit on the strips of paper.

• Glue paper strips to cover the sides of the box lid (see sketch).

• Punch two holes on sides of box opposite each other, two inches from corner (see sketch).

• Thread long ribbons through holes opposite each other. Secure with knots at each end.

• Tie ribbons together in the middle with shorter ribbon to make handle (see sketch).

Simplification Idea: Provide stickers for children to put on box sides. Or cut out magazine pictures of flowers, vegetables and fruit for children to glue to strips of paper.

Enrichment Idea: Child letters "I am a faithful helper" on one side of box.

Conversation Suggestions: **What does the word faithful mean?** (Reliable, trustworthy, honest.) **How can you be a faithful helper at home? How could you use your basket to be a good helper?** (To serve a snack to a friend, bring flowers, vegetables or fruit in from the garden, carry in the newspaper or the mail, etc.) **The Bible says all people should learn to be faithful—moms and dads, teachers, boys and girls, too.**

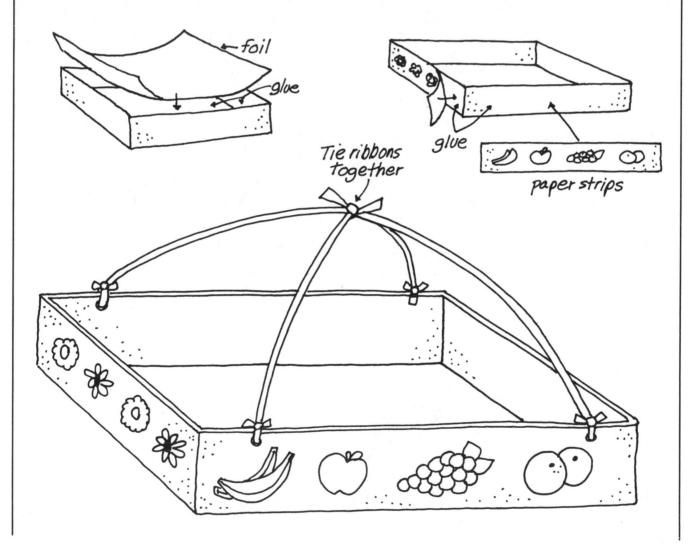

foil

glue

Tie ribbons together

glue

paper strips

"Treat Me Gentle" Finger Puppet

Materials: Black fine-tip permanent pens, pink and blue ⅛-inch ribbon, yarn, construction paper, crayons, glue, hole punch, scissors, colored tissue paper, skewer, bowl. For each child—one egg, one white lunch-size paper bag, two tiny black pom-poms. (NOTE: In case of accidents, make available additional eggs.)

Preparation: Poke a wooden or metal skewer into the larger end of each egg, then widen the hole until is is large enough for a child's finger. Drain eggs into bowl. Rinse shells and let dry thoroughly. (Remember to use the eggs' "insides" for your cooking needs.) Cut ribbon into 4-inch (10-cm) lengths and tie into small bows—one for each child. Cut yarn into 12-inch (30-cm) lengths—one for each child. Cut tissue paper into small squares.

Instruct each child in the following procedures:

• Holding eggshell on one finger, use a permanent pen to draw mouth, nose, ears, eyebrows, etc. (sketch a).

• Glue pom-poms in place for eyes.

• Glue bow on top of head or at neck.

• Cut bag half way from the top into scallop or zig-zag shapes (sketch b). Decorate bag with crayons.

• Crinkle pieces of tissue paper and place inside bag for puppet's "bed".

• Punch a hole in the center top of both sides of bag (sketch c).

• Insert one end of a piece of yarn through each hole and tie to form handle.

• Place eggshell finger puppet in bag.

Enrichment Idea: Photocopy the following poem onto small pieces of paper. Child punches a hole in the paper and ties it to bag with yarn.

GUESS WHAT I AM!
I'm usually white.
I'm oval and small.
I'll break if you toss me,
I'm not a ball!
Be gentle with me,
Or I'm nothing at all!

Conversation Suggestions: **What will happen to your egg puppet if you are too rough with it? How should you handle your egg? God wants us to learn to be gentle and careful. When you get home, read the poem to your friends and family. Then ask them to guess what's inside your bag.**

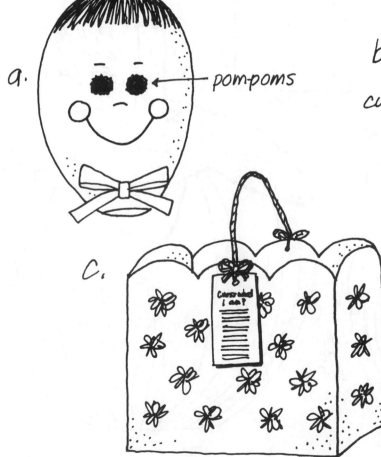

Strawberry Cookie Jar

Materials: Tacky glue, fiber fill, red tissue paper, green felt, scissors, tagboard. For each child—a 2-pound coffee can.

Preparation: Use tagboard to make several leaf patterns. Cut a 6-inch (15-cm) tagboard circle for each child. Cut tissue paper into 24-inch (60-cm) squares—one for each child. Cut 4×5-inch (10×12.5-cm) felt rectangles—one for each child.

Instruct each child in the following procedures:

• Glue fiber fill around upper third of coffee can (sketch a).

• Lay tissue paper out flat and set coffee can in the center of the paper.

• Put a line of glue around inside rim of can.

• Gather edges of paper and bring up loosely to cover coffee can. (Batting will give a rounded, strawberry-shaped appearance.)

• Fold paper over rim of coffee can and press firmly, securing edges on line of glue.

• Trace leaf pattern onto large piece of felt and cut out.

• To make lid for cookie jar, glue tagboard circle to center of felt leaf.

• With circle on the underneath side, secure lid by gluing one point of leaf to tissue paper (sketch b).

• Cut slits along one long side of small felt rectangle (sketch c).

• With slits at the bottom, roll felt to make stem and glue to hold together.

• Fan out "fringes" and glue stem to lid (sketch d). Let dry.

Enrichment Idea: Have children letter "The Fruit of the Spirit is . . . self-control" on inside of lid before attaching to can.

Conversation Suggestions: **What is self-control?** (Not letting yourself do something that hurts you or others.) **If your cookie jar was full of your favorite cookies, how could you show self-control? Eating too many cookies might hurt your body. When you only eat a few you are showing self-control. Name some other ways you can control yourself.**

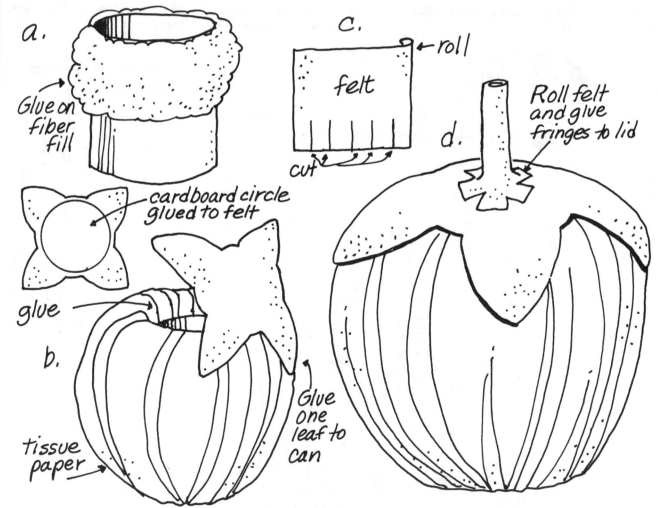

a. Glue on fiber fill

cardboard circle glued to felt

glue

b.

tissue paper

c. felt — roll cut

d. Roll felt and glue fringes to lid

Glue one leaf to can

Leaf Pattern for Strawberry Cookie Jar

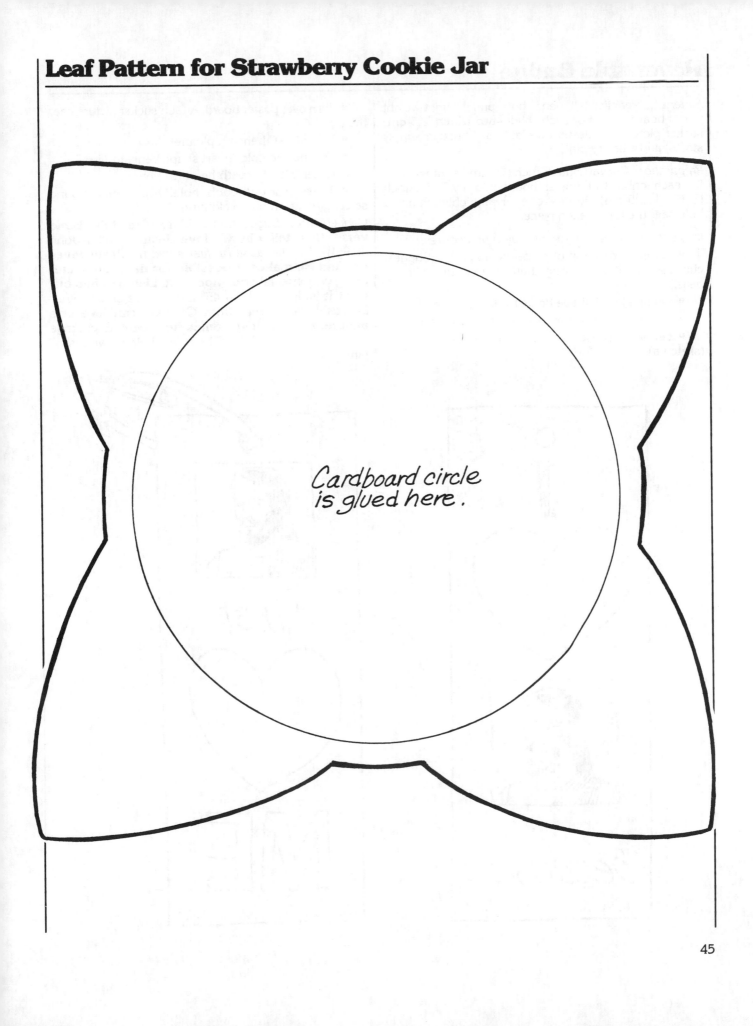

Cardboard circle is glued here.

Reversible Badge

Materials: Pencils, felt pens, hole punch, light-weight poster board, yarn. For each child—two 1-inch (2.5-cm) sticker pictures of Jesus (available at Christian supply stores) and a safety pin.

Preparation: Cut yarn into 6-inch (15-cm) lengths—one for each child. Cut poster board into 1½ × 4½-inch (3.75 × 11.25-cm) pieces—one for each child. Punch a hole near the top of each piece.

Instruct each child in the following procedures:

• Letter "I" near top of poster board piece. (Suggest child use pencil for lettering, then trace lettering with felt pens.)

• Outline heart shape beneath "I." Color heart.

• Attach sticker picture of Jesus beneath heart.

• Letter "because . . . " at bottom of poster board (sketch a).

• Turn over poster board. Attach sticker picture near the top.

• Letter "first" beneath picture.

• Outline and color heart shape beneath "first."

• Letter "ME" beneath heart (sketch b).

• Thread yarn through hole. Knot ends around safety pin. Attach pin to clothing.

Conversation Suggestions: **Listen to this Bible verse, then tell why we love Jesus.** Read 1 John 4:19: *We love because he first loved us.* **Jesus loves us. And He makes it possible for us to do something very special and important. Listen to find out what it is.** Read 1 John 4:7: *Let us love one another because loves comes from God.* **We can love one another because love comes from God.** Encourage children to repeat 1 John 4:19, using their "I Love Jesus" pins.

Money Bag

Materials: Vinyl or suede fabric, scissors, plastic lacing or yarn, awl or ice pick, permanent markers. Optional—hammers, large nails, blocks of wood.

Preparation: Cut vinyl into 8-inch (20-cm) circles—one for each child. Punch holes at regular intervals near edge of each circle (sketch a). Cut lacing into 36-inch (90-cm) lengths—one for each child.

Instruct each child in the following procedures:

- Decorate one side of fabric circle with felt markers.
- Run lacing in and out of holes (sketch a), gathering circle into a bag (sketch b).
- Tie ends of lacing together in a knot.

Enrichment Idea: Instead of teacher punching holes, children place fabric on block of wood and tap holes around edge of circle using hammer and nail.

Conversation Suggestions: **Why do you think we give gifts of money to our** (Sunday School, church, vacation Bible school)**? We give our money gift because we love God and Jesus and want to help others know about Jesus.** Talk with children about how your (Sunday School) uses the money it receives. **The next time you bring your money gift, you can bring it in your Money Bag.**

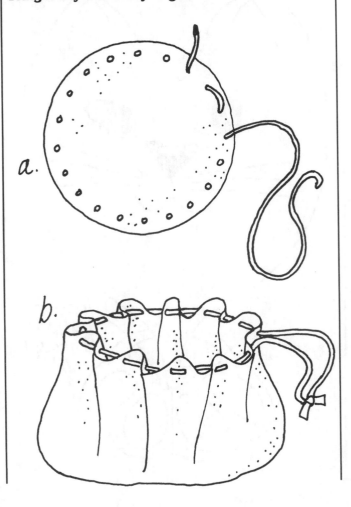

Water Watcher

Materials: Glue, cotton, feathers, fake fur or yarn. For each child—one bamboo skewer (available in grocery stores), two small wiggle eyes, one dry seed pod about the size of a walnut (small Styrofoam ball, pinecone or peach seed can also be used).

Preparation: Use an ice pick or electric drill to make a small hole in the bottom of each seed pod just big enough to insert the skewer.

Instruct each child in the following procedures:

- Glue wiggle eyes to the pod.
- Glue feathers, fake fur or yarn to top of pod for hair (sketch a).
- When dry, fill the hole in pod with glue.
- Insert skewer into pod (sketch b). If necessary, wrap a small piece of cotton around the blunt end of the skewer before inserting to keep skewer secure in hole in pod. Let dry.
- "Water Watcher" is inserted into the soil of a potted houseplant. Child may pull out and check the stick and when it looks dry, water the plant.

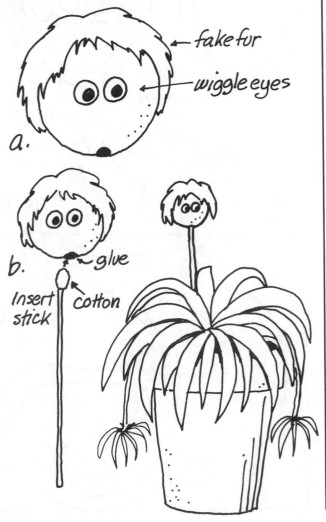

Balloon Animals

Materials: Poster board, permanent felt markers, hole punch, scissors. For each child—large round balloon.

Preparation: Provide examples of various animal footprints—webbed, hooves, paws, etc. (sketch a). Cut poster board into 4 × 6-inch (10. × 15.-cm) rectangles—one for each child.

Instruct each child in the following procedures:

• Choose a footprint. Draw, then cut footprint from poster board rectangle. (Footprint should be large, using most of the rectangle to support balloon.)

• Draw an *X* in the middle of the foot.

• Cut a slit to the *X* and punch hole in center of *X* (sketch b).

• Inflate balloon and tie a knot (assist children as necessary).

• Use slit to slide knot of balloon to hole in foot (sketch c).

• With felt markers, draw facial features of animal on balloon.

Simplification Idea: Children mix up footprints and balloons and play matching game instead of inserting balloon in footprint base.

Conversation Suggestions: As children work, ask, **Which animals have paws? Hooves? Webbed feet? Why do** (cats) **need paws?** (Horses) **need hooves?** (Ducks) **need webbed feet? What kind of feet do people have? What things can people do with their feet?** (Climb, stand, jump, etc.)

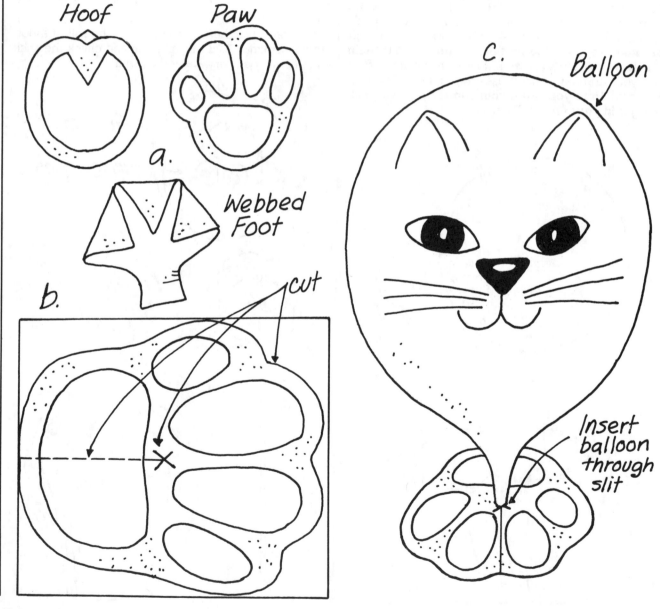

Cardboard Tube Butterfly

Materials: Construction paper in assorted colors, string, tape, scissors, glue, hole punch, felt pens or paint and paintbrushes. For each child—cardboard tube (approximately 5-inches (12.5-cm) long), one chenille wire.

Preparation: Fold construction paper, place patterns on fold and cut 1 large and 1 small set of wings—one set for each butterfly. Cut string into 36-inch (90-cm) lengths)—one for each child.

Instruct each child in the following procedures:
- Decorate the tube with felt pens or paint.
- Glue center section of the small set of wings to the center of the large set (sketch a).
- Cut or tear small pieces of paper and glue them to the wings for decoration.
- Glue the center part of the wings to the tube (sketch b).
- Punch two circles from black construction paper and glue in place for eyes.
- Bend a chenille wire to make antennae for butterfly. Glue to tube or push wire through cardboard to secure.
- Bend the top ends of wire into spirals.
- Punch hole in tube. Thread one end of string through hole and tie ends of string together (this makes loop for easy holding).

Large wing pattern

Small wing pattern

Place on fold

Glue small butterfly to large butterfly

a.

b.

chenille wire

glue to tube

Clothes Hanger Face Mask

Materials: Glue, scraps of felt and yarn, ribbon and fake fur. For each child—a wire coat hanger, one nylon hose leg cut from pantyhose.

Preparation: Cut the legs from pantyhose to make two full length stockings. Do this for each pair of pantyhose.

Instruct each child in the following procedures:

- Bend the coat hanger into an oval, round or diamond shape.
- Bend the end of the hook into a loop (sketch a).
- Pull the nylon over the large oval.
- Twist the end of the stocking and tie securely.
- Cut facial features from felt and glue in place. Cut and glue on yarn hair.

Conversation Suggestions: As children complete masks, say, **Let's play 'What would you do if . . . '** Briefly describe an everyday situation in which a child must make a decision. For example, **Brian, what would you do if Stephanie wanted to go to the park without asking first?** Ask volunteers to use masks as they dramatize the situation. Let other children take turns to act out their responses. Continue with similar situations as time and interest allow. Ask, **Why do we want to do things that are right and good?** (Because we love God and want to obey His Word.)

Bend hanger

a.

Make loop

b.

Engraved Bible Verse

Materials: Lightweight cardboard, heavy duty aluminum foil, glue, water, shallow containers, paste brushes, scissors, old ball-point pens (without ink), magnetic tape.

Preparation: Cut magnetic tape into 1-inch (2.5-cm) pieces—two for each child. Cut cardboard into 2×6-inch (5×15-cm) pieces—one for each child. Cut foil into 3×7-inch (7.5×17.5-cm) pieces—one for each child. Thin glue with water until mixture is easy to spread with brush. Pour into containers. Make several unmarked samples of engraving pads, following procedure described below.

Instruct each child in the following procedures:

- Using brush, spread glue on top of cardboard.
- Place foil, shiny side down, on glue covered cardboard (sketch a).
- Wrap foil edges around cardboard and smooth until flattened.
- Practice writing or drawing with ball-point pen on sample pads provided. (Caution child not to push too hard with the ball-point pen.) Say, **If you want to make your letters deeper, go over them again with the pen.**
- "Engrave" a verse on pad using ball-point pen (sketch b). (Discuss and then select brief verses. E.g., *God loves you; Love one another; God sent His Son; Love is patient.*)
- Adhere magnetic strips to back of cardboard.

Conversation Suggestions: **When you hear the word "love," what do you think of? What do you think is the difference between loving someone and liking something** (bike riding, swimming, favorite food)**?** Listen carefully to children's responses. **The kind of love God has for us and the kind of love He wants us to show others means always doing what is best for others.**

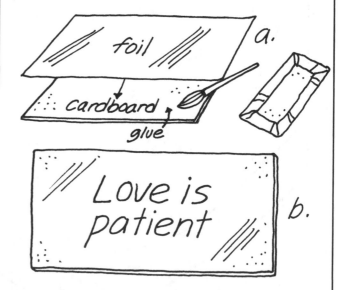

foil   a.

cardboard

glue

Love is patient   b.

Bouncy Person

Materials: Hole punch, colored art feathers (optional), scissors, permanent felt pens, chalkboard and chalk. For each child—one clean Styrofoam meat tray, six rubber bands.

Preparation: Draw body part shapes (sketch a) on chalkboard, showing where to punch holes.

Instruct each child in the following procedures:

• Cut body shapes (head, body, arms and legs) from foam trays.

• Draw facial features on head shape.

• Referring to chalkboard, punch holes in appropriate places to join body parts (sketch a).

• Cut the rubber bands. Fasten body parts together by inserting rubber bands through holes and tying ends securely (sketch b).

• Make hole in top of the head and tie a rubber band so that it forms a loop for holding.

• Insert feathers into Stryofoam around the edge of the head.

• Bounce Bouncy Person up and down.

Conversation Suggestions: **What is your favorite game to play at recess? What do you need to be a soccer player? What parts of your body do you use to play that game?** Help children to think of strong legs and good eyesight as gifts from God. **Your Bouncy Person reminds us that God has made our bodies so we can run and jump. I'm glad, aren't you?**

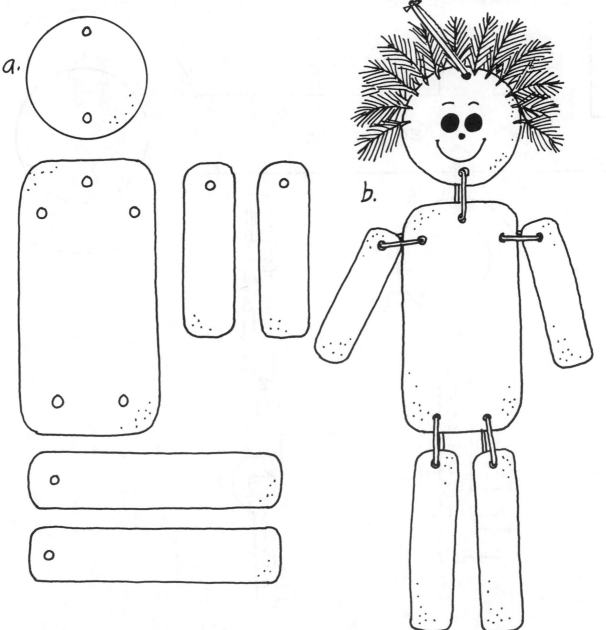

Friendship Key Chain

Materials: Colored construction paper, glue, paste brushes, shallow containers, water, lightweight cardboard, felt pens, pencils.

Preparation: Make several key patterns. Use paper cutter to cut ¾ × 5-inch (1.9 × 12.5-cm) strips—eight for each child. Thin glue with water until mixture is easy to spread with brush. Pour into containers.

Instruct each child in the following procedures:

• Trace key pattern onto construction paper and cut out.

• Letter "Love one another" on key (sketch a).

• Draw a different friend's face on each of four paper strips.

• Assemble chain, by gluing paper strips together so that faces show (sketch b).

• Thread last strip through key then add to other links of chain.

Conversation Suggestions: As children work, ask questions to help them select the friends they wish to draw. **Why is** (Trista) **your special friend? What do you like about your friend** (Kurt)**? What do you like to do together? Have you ever helped your friend? How? Our Bible says,** *Friends love one another* (see Proverbs 17:17).

Key Pattern

a.

b.

Love one another

VIP Badge

Materials: Construction paper, 1-inch (2.5-cm) wide satin ribbon, cardboard, straight pins, felt pens, scissors, glue, pencil.

Preparation: Cut ribbon into 12-inch (30-cm) lengths—one for each child. From cardboard, cut two circle patterns, one 3-inches (7.5-cm) in diameter, the other 1½-inches (3.75-cm) in diameter.

Instruct each child in the following procedures:

• Use patterns and construction paper to make two circles of contrasting size and color.

• Glue the smaller circle in the center of the larger one.

• Choose someone who is a Very Important Person to you. Letter name around outside of larger circle (sketch a).

• Letter "You are a VIP" in the smaller circle.

• Fold ribbon in half and glue to back of badge (sketch b). Place a pin in the badge (for attaching badge to your VIP.)

Conversation Suggestions: **What do the initials VIP stand for?** (Very Important Person). **Let's think about some people who are very important to you** (parents, grandparents, school and Sunday School teachers, friends, librarian, etc.). **What are some ways these people care for you? Did you know that God made these special people to help care for you? He did! God loves you very much.**

Seat Belt Reminder

Materials: Felt pens. For each child—a plain adhesive-backed label, at least 2 × 3-inches (5 × 7.5-cm) (available at stationery or variety stores).

Instruct each child in the following procedures:

• Decide on a slogan to remind car passengers and driver to fasten seat belts before traveling in the car ("Buckle up," "Fasten your seat belt!")

• Use felt pens to letter slogan on sticker.

• Decorate with colorful designs.

• Attach sticker to dashboard of family car. (Remind children to ask parent's permission.)

Conversation Suggestions: **Why do you think you need to wear a seat belt? What might happen if you don't wear one? What has God given you to help you remember important things? God has made your mind so you can think and remember. God wants you to use your mind!**

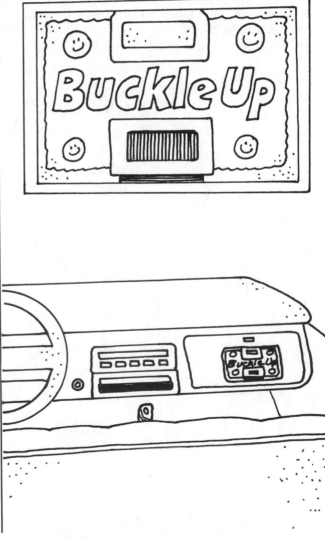

"Thank You, God" Wall Hanging
(A Two-Day Project)

Materials: Burlap in assorted colors (tight weave), dried seeds (such as red, black and white beans, split peas, apple and orange seeds), pasta in a variety of shapes, wrapping paper scraps, lightweight cardboard, red and orange construction paper, felt pens, scissors, hole punch, pencils, yarn, glue.

Preparation: Cut yarn into 48-inch (120-cm) lengths—one for each child. Cut burlap into 8 × 10-inch (20 × 25-cm) pieces—three pieces for each child. Cut fruit and paper doll patterns from cardboard. Cut wrapping paper into 6 × 7-inch (15 × 17.5-cm) pieces.

Instruct each child in the following procedures:

• Using felt pen, letter "Thank You, God" across one piece of burlap.

• Trace fruit patterns onto construction paper and cut out.

• Glue paper fruit onto second burlap piece.

• Arrange and then glue seeds onto paper fruit (sketch a).

• Arrange and glue beans, peas and pasta in a flower or geometric design.

• Fold wrapping paper piece in half (sketch b).

• Trace Paper Doll Pattern onto folded paper. Cut out.

• Trace and cut out several more paper dolls (number in child's family) and glue to third piece of burlap.

• Punch holes in each piece of burlap (sketch a).

• Thread yarn through holes, allowing extra length at the top for a hanger.

• Tie ends of yarn through holes of bottom burlap piece. Let dry.

Conversation Suggestions: **What are your favorite foods? What is used to make** (pizza)**? Where does the** (cheese, tomatoes) **come from?** Ask questions to help children understand that everything they have comes from God's creation. Talk about the members of each child's family. **Who are the people God has planned to care for you?** Be sure no child feels his/her family situation is unacceptable to you. **There are many kinds of families. Some have two people in them. Some have more. How many are in the family God has given you? Our Wall Hangings help us remember to thank God for the good things He has given us.**

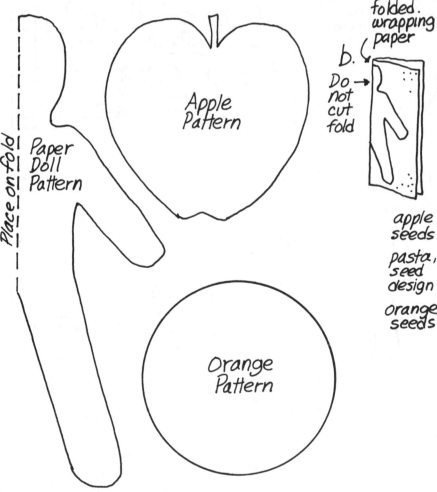

54

Pop-Up Puppet

Materials: Felt pens, yarn, glue, pencil. For each child— a 1-inch (2.5-cm) Styrofoam ball, a paper towel tube, a plastic straw or bamboo skewer. Optional—unwaxed paper cups may be used instead of paper towel tubes.

Preparation: Cut yarn into small pieces. Cut paper towel tubes to 6-inch (15-cm) length.

Instruct each child in the following procedures:

• With felt pen, draw facial features on Styrofoam ball.

• Glue bits of yarn onto Styrofoam ball for hair.

• Use a pencil to carefully make a hole in the bottom of Styrofoam ball. (If using skewers instead of straws, use skewer to make hole.)

• Place glue on end of straw and in hole. Insert straw (or skewer) into hole (sketch a).

• Use felt pens to draw clothing details on cardboard tube.

• Insert straw through tube (sketch b).

Enrichment Idea: Children dress puppets with felt clothes they cut out.

Conversation Suggestions: Children use puppets to act out ways of showing kindness. Suggest, **Kevin, let's pretend Susan is your little sister. She comes into your room where you've very carefully built a race track for your cars. She wants to play with you, but you know she might mess up the cars and track. Use your puppet to show us what you would do.** Then ask other children how they would show kindness in this and similar everyday situations.

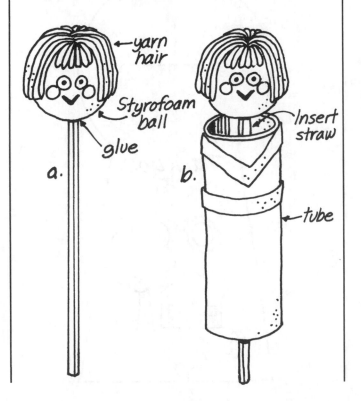

Seasons Wheel

Materials: White poster board, felt pens, black construction paper, paper fasteners, rulers, pencils.

Preparation: Cut 12-inch (30-cm) circles from poster board—one for each child. On chalkboard, letter: *As long as the earth remains, there will be springtime and harvest, cold and heat, winter and summer, day and night* (see Genesis 8:22).

Instruct each child in the following procedures:

• Using ruler and pencil, divide circle into four sections (sketch a).

• Use felt pens to draw items to illustrate the four seasons—one season in each section. (Summer—sun, fruit; winter—snowman; spring—rain, flowers, umbrella; fall—leaves.) Optional—cut items from construction paper.

• Cut a pointer from black construction paper.

• Attach pointer to center of circle with paper fastener (sketch b).

• Around outer edge of circle, letter Spring, Summer, Fall, Winter in the appropriate sections.

• Turn pointer to current season.

Conversation Suggestions: **What is a promise? We have a special promise from God in this Bible verse. Let's read it together on the chalkboard and find out.** All read verse. **What is the promise? Is God doing what He promised? How do you know? God always does what He promises. We can count on it!**

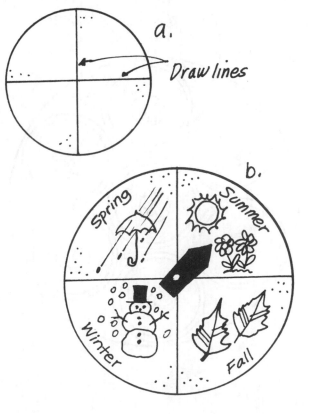

Trivet

Materials: Spray paint in a variety of colors, glue, felt, colorful self-adhesive stickers, lightweight cardboard, scissors. For each child—seven baby food jar lids. Optional—old shirts or paint smocks.

Preparation: Spray paint baby food jar lids in a variety of colors. (Two day option—children may paint lids with acrylic paint and a small paintbrush. Be sure painters wear smocks as acrylic paint does not completely wash out. Allow paint to dry overnight.) Make several cardboard patterns for a 6-inch (15-cm) circle.

Instruct each child in the following procedures:

- Choose seven painted lids.
- Decorate top of each lid with a colorful sticker.
- Trace circle pattern onto felt and cut out.
- Glue lids to felt circle (see sketch). Let dry thoroughly overnight.

Conversation Suggestions: **Does your mother set a hot dish directly on the table? Why does she put something under the hot dish? Your trivet will help keep the heat away from the table. Why do we give gifts like this trivet to someone?** (To show our love.) **Who could you show love to with this gift?**

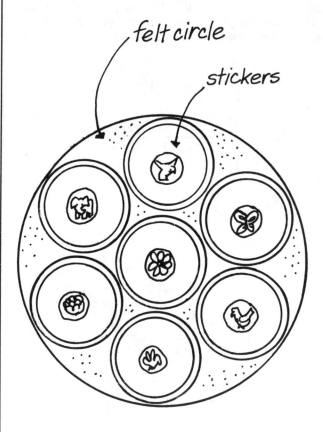

felt circle

stickers

Doorknob Prayer Reminder

Materials: Felt, glue, water, shallow containers, paste brushes, scissors, felt pens, construction paper, lightweight cardboard, pencils, yarn.

Preparation: Trace outline of doorknob pattern onto cardboard and cut out. Trace cardboard pattern onto felt and cut out—one for each child. (Optional—have each child cut out felt piece.) Cut slits in each doorknob hanger. Thin glue with water so mixture spreads easily with brush. Pour glue into containers.

Instruct each child in the following procedures:

- Letter "Thank You, God" on felt (see pattern).
- Cut out items to be thankful for (flowers, food, family, home, clothes, sun, stars, trees, etc.) from felt scraps or construction paper.
- Glue items to doorknob hanger.

Conversation Suggestions: To stimulate children's thinking about prayer, ask, **What do you like to talk to God about? What do you thank Him for? What do you say when you thank Him? When I have a problem, I tell God about it and ask Him to help me. Do you sometimes ask for God's help? We also like to praise God by telling Him just how great and good He is. You can put your Prayer Reminder on your bedroom doorknob to help you remember to talk to God before you go to sleep or when you wake up.** Ask a child to demonstrate placing hanger over a doorknob in your classroom.

Thank you, God

**Doorknob
Prayer
Reminder
Pattern**

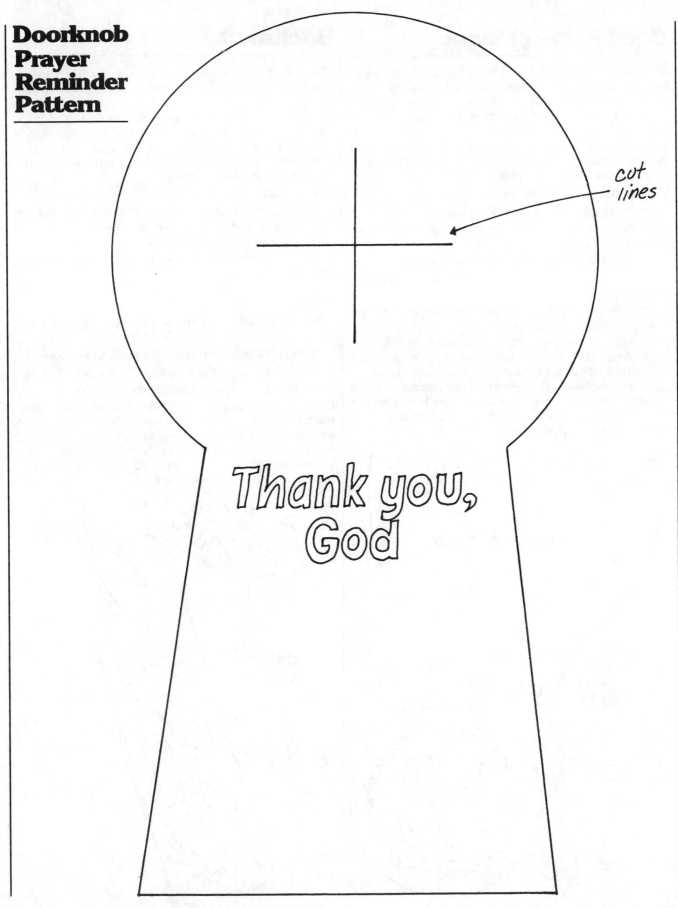

cut
lines

Thank you,
God

57

Seed Flower Plaque

Materials: Glue, water, shallow containers, paste brushes, hole punch, assorted seeds (cantaloupe, sunflower, apple, pumpkin, watermelon, beans, green), chenille wires, lightweight cardboard, scissors, yarn. For each child—paper plate.

Preparation: Make a flower pattern with cardboard. Cut yarn into 10-inch (25-cm) lengths. Trace the flower pattern near the top of each plate.

Instruct each child in the following procedures:

• Brush glue inside the flower outline.

• Outline and then fill in the flower with seeds (sketch a).

• Decorate the rim of the plate with seeds.

• Glue the chenille wires in place for flower stem and leaves.

• Punch holes at top of plate. Thread yarn through holes for hanger (sketch b).

Conversation Suggestions: Ask questions to help children name the foods from which the seeds came. Then ask, **Which seeds do we eat?** (Beans, peas, sunflower.) **Why do you think God planned for plants to have seeds? What do seeds need to grow into plants? God has promised to send sun and rain so our food will grow.** (See Genesis 8:22.)

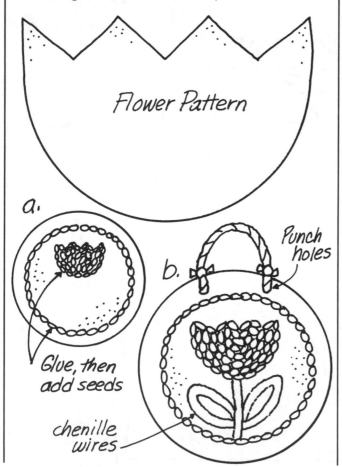

Flower Pattern

a.

Glue, then add seeds

Punch holes

b.

chenille wires

Bookmark

Materials: Broken crayons, hand held pencil sharpener, waxed paper, hole punch, yarn, scissors, electric iron, newspapers.

Preparation: Cut waxed paper into 2×6-inch (5×15-cm) pieces—two for each child. Cut yarn into 6-inch (15-cm) lengths—one for each child. Remove paper from crayon pieces. Cover work area with newspapers. Preheat iron at "wool" setting.

Instruct each child in the following procedures:

• Use pencil sharpener to grate assorted colors from crayons onto one piece of waxed paper. Keep crayon shavings away from edges of paper.

• Place other strip of waxed paper directly over the first strip.

• Carefully cover with a layer of newspaper and press with iron until crayons melt.

• Let cool and then trim any uneven edges of bookmark.

• Punch a hole near top of bookmark (see sketch).

• Thread a length of yarn through the hole and tie.

• Unravel the ends of yarn to form a tassel.

Conversation Suggestions: **Why do we use bookmarks?** Show your Bible in which you've inserted a bookmark at a favorite verse. Demonstrate using the bookmark. Read Bible verse. When bookmarks are completed, help each child locate a familiar verse in his/her Bible, then insert bookmark.

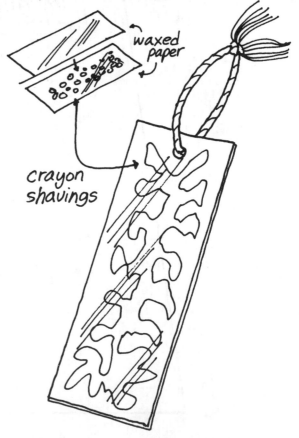

waxed paper

crayon shavings

Turtle Tub Puppet

Materials: Green construction paper, transparent tape, scissors, black, green and brown permanent felt pens (pens used for marking transparencies work well), craft knife. For each child—one small, clean white margarine tub with lid.

Instruct each child in the following procedures:

• Remove the lid from the tub, place on a sheet of green construction paper and trace around it.

• Remove the lid then draw the head, legs and tail on the body and cut out (sketch a).

• Place the cutout piece on top of the tub and carefully press on the lid (sketch b).

• Straighten out the head, legs and tail.

• Use felt pens to decorate the shell (bottom of tub) and to make the eyes.

• Teacher uses knife to cut two parallel lines, about 2-inches (5.-cm) long and 1-inch (2.5-cm) apart, through the lid and the paper (sketch c).

• Slip your finger through the slits and use as a puppet (sketch d).

Conversation Suggestions: **Of all the animals God has made, which one do you think is prettiest? Feels softest? Runs fastest? Makes the loudest sound? Has the longest tail? I really enjoy watching animals, don't you? Our Bible tells us that God *... gives us all things to enjoy.*** (See 1 Timothy 6:17.)

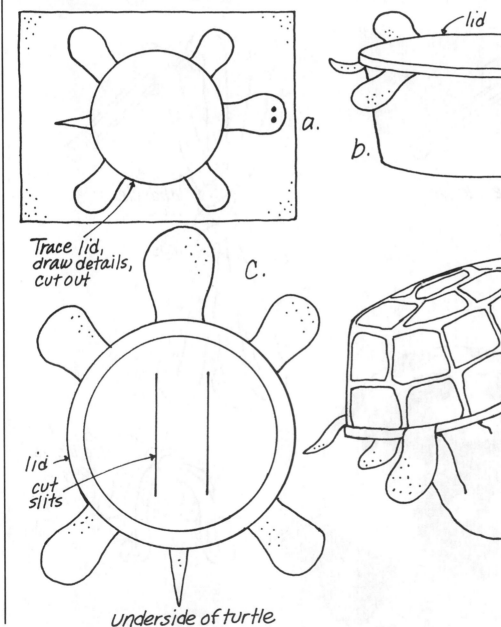

Trace lid, draw details, cut out

a.

b.

lid

c.

lid
cut
slits

underside of turtle

d.

Lady Bug

Materials: Red enamel spray paint, black felt pen, black chenille wires, black pom-poms, glue; for each child—the round end of a plastic egg-shaped pantyhose container. (Optional—large paper clips, black self-adhesive dots).

Preparation: Paint the round end of plastic pantyhose containers with red spray paint. Let dry at least 24 hours.

Instruct each child in the following procedures:

- Use black felt pen (or self-adhesive dots) to make dots on bug's body.
- Bend a chenille wire in half, forming small loop (sketch a).
- Twist ends of wire around pencil to make antennae.

- Glue loop in chenille wire antennae to body, then glue black pom-pom head to loop (sketch b). (Tip: A large paper clip will hold antennae and head in place until glue dries.)
- Twist the centers of three chenille wires together then curl ends over pencil to form legs and feet (sketch c). (For younger children, teacher may want to twist wires together ahead of time.)
- Glue twisted portion of wires to inside of body. Hold in place for several minutes until glue sets. Then spread wires apart to form legs.

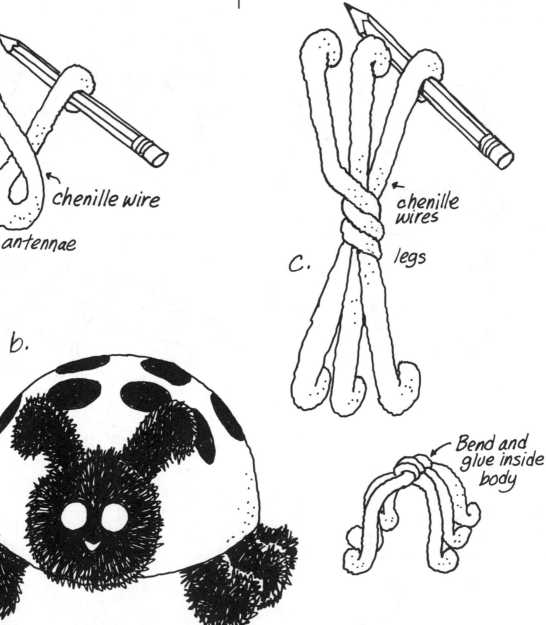

a. chenille wire
antennae

b.

c. chenille wires legs

Bend and glue inside body

Beanbag
(A Two-Day Project)

Materials: Scissors, felt scraps, glue, lentils, lightweight cardboard, scissors, pencils. Optional—needles, thread.

Preparation: Cut several circle patterns from cardboard.

Instruct each child in the following procedures:

• Use pattern to cut two circles of the same size from felt.

• Decorate one or both circles by gluing on felt cut-outs (sketch a).

• Squeeze glue around the edge of the back side of one circle leaving about one inch of the edge unglued for an opening.

• Place the second circle over the glued circle and press together with hands.

• Let dry overnight.

• Spoon dried lentils into the opening of the glued circles (sketch b). Fill half full.

• Glue opening together and press with hands.

Enrichment Idea: Instead of gluing, children sew around edges of felt to finish beanbag.

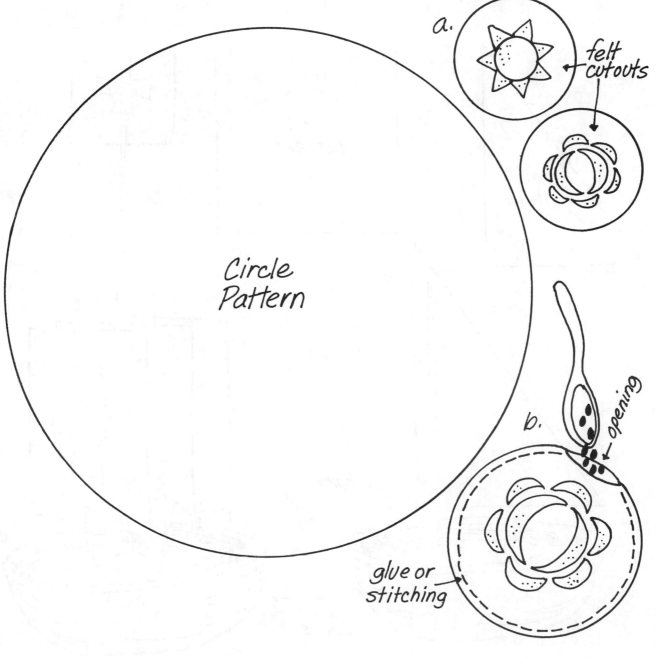

a.

felt cutouts

Circle Pattern

b.

opening

glue or stitching

Walnut Ships

Materials: Non-hardening clay, scissors, colored construction paper, white glue, toothpicks, felt markers or crayons. For each child—one walnut shell half.
Instruct each child in the following procedures:

Sailboat:

- Press a small ball of clay into walnut shell half.
- Cut a small triangular sail from the construction paper.
- Glue the sail to a toothpick leaving enough toothpick at the bottom to push into the clay (sketch a). Let dry.
- Push toothpick into clay.

Clipper Ship:

- Cut three small squares from construction paper.
- Draw a design on one square with felt markers or crayons.
- Push toothpicks through the tops and bottoms of each sail (sketch b) leaving enough toothpick mast at the bottom to push into the clay.
- Push toothpicks into clay (sketch c).

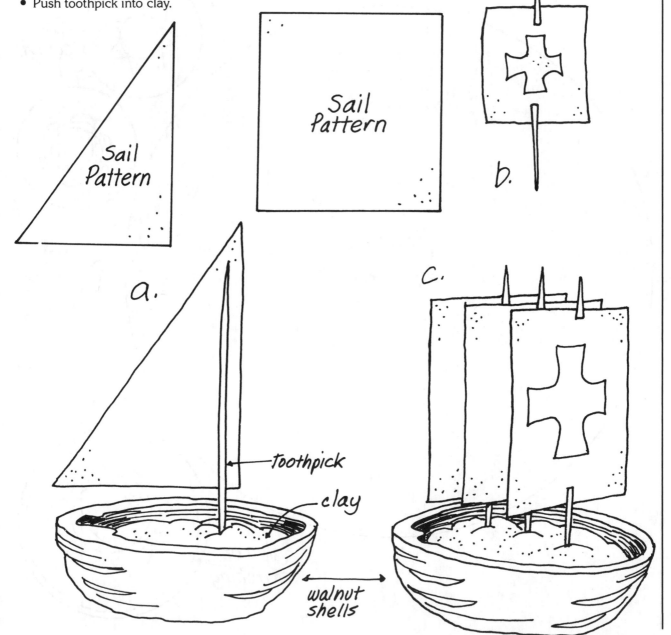

Sail Pattern

Sail Pattern

b.

a.

c.

toothpick

clay

walnut shells

Crafts for Older Elementary

Trying to plan craft projects for older children has driven many teachers prematurely grey. The challenge is that while these children have well-developed skills to complete projects, they also have well-developed preferences about what they want to do. Thus a project that may challenge their abilities may be scorned because it somehow is not appealing to these young sophisticates. Then the next project will seem juvenile to the adult, but will click with the kids!

There's no justice! And a sense of humor surely helps. One helpful device is to filter a craft idea through a panel of experts—two or three sixth graders. If they like it, chances are the rest of the group will, also. Then, the better you get to know your particular students, the better your batting average will be.

And most of the time, most of the group will thoroughly enjoy the projects in this section. They have been tested under fire and came out with colors flying and only a few tatters.

Egg Shell Scene

Materials: Fine-tipped paintbrushes, several needles, sharp-pointed scissors, several colors of acrylic paint, clear acrylic spray, small bowls, paper clips, newspapers, paper towels. For each student—one or more raw eggs.

Preparation: Cover work area with newspapers.

Instruct each student in the following procedures:

- With a needle, make a hole in both ends of egg (sketch a).
- Slightly enlarge hole in bigger end of egg with needle or scissors.
- Holding egg over bowl, blow carefully on small hole to force egg out of shell through larger hole.
- Rinse shell and gently pat dry with paper towel.
- Straighten paper clip enough to insert into shell (sketch b).
- Holding egg by paper clip, paint scene on egg shell (sketch c shows an example depicting one aspect of creation).
- Let dry for a few minutes, then spray with clear acrylic finish to seal and protect.

Enrichment Idea: Using a branch of a tree or a wire or string hung across part of the room, have students hang their eggs up for display.

Conversation Suggestions: Guide student in deciding on illustration for egg. Ask questions to connect the student's design to your lesson emphasis. For example, **What things did God create first? Next? What part of God's creation are you most thankful for?**

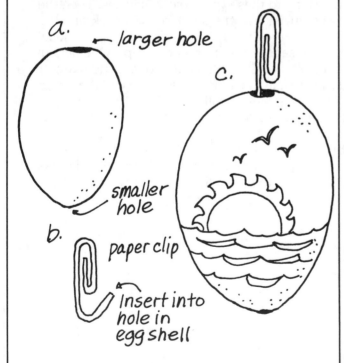

Pom-pom Plaque

Materials: Heavy cardboard, scissors, glue, rickrack, hole punch, yarn. For each student—one dark blue 8½ × 11-inch (21.5 × 27.5-cm) felt square, 60½-inch (1.25-cm) light-colored pom-poms in a variety of light colors.

Preparation: For each student—cut cardboard to measure 8½ × 11-inches (21.5 × 27.5-cm); cut rickrack into two 11-inch (27.5-cm) and two 8½-inch (21.5-cm) lengths; cut yarn into one 10-inch (25-cm) length.

Instruct each student in the following procedures:

- Glue felt to cardboard.
- Use pom-poms to form lesson-related words and/or designs on felt (sketch a).
- Glue pom-poms in place.
- Glue rickrack around edge of felt to make a border.
- Punch a hole near each end at top of picture.
- Thread a piece of yarn through each of the holes and secure with a knot (sketch b).

Conversation suggestions: If your lesson deals with the subject of God's love, you could say, **God loves us so much that He sent Jesus to earth to die for our sins. What can we put on our plaques to remind us of God's love?** (Cross, heart, the word LOVE, etc.) Encourage students to think of creative ideas. **When you hang your picture up it will help you to remember to thank God for His love.**

Joy Fella

Materials: Knife, pencil, glue, scissors, red and blue acrylic or enamel paint, paintbrushes. For each student—one grapefruit, a 2-oz. plastic cup, a large rubber band, two 1-inch (2.5-cm) pom-poms, one ½-inch (1.25-cm) pom-pom, two small wiggle eyes.

Preparation: At least a week ahead of time, teacher cuts grapefruit in half and scoops out pulp. With a pencil, punch a hole ½ inch from edge of each half of grapefruit (sketch a). Make grapefruit juice out of the pulp. Let peels dry 7 to 10 days.

Instruct each student in the following procedures:

• Paint outside rim of grapefruit with red paint to highlight "lips."

• Paint the cup blue. Optional—letter a lesson-related word (e.g., JOY) on the cup (turned bottom up) with red paint. Allow to dry.

• Push the rubber band through both of the holes in grapefruit.

• Knot ends of rubber band to make a hinge (sketch b). Child may need help from teacher.

• Glue on pom-poms for eyes and nose.

• Glue wiggle eyes on pom-pom eyes.

• Glue cup to top of grapefruit "head" for hat (sketch c).

• Allow paint and glue to dry thoroughly.

Enrichment Idea: Children may glue Joy Fella to poster board or plywood base and label with lesson-related words such as "The fruit of the Spirit is joy."

Conversation Suggestions: Encourage students to use their finished crafts as puppets to repeat a Bible verse or other lesson-related phrase to each other. Talk with students about the day's lesson. For example, **Why is it nice to be around a joyful person? We all like friends who make us feel happy. Our Joy Fella can be a friendly reminder that *the fruit of the Spirit is joy.***

a.

b.

rubber band hinge

c.

The fruit of the Spirit is JOY!

Peaceful Hand Memo Holder

Materials: Yarn, 1/8-inch elastic (the kind used in sewing), fiber fill stuffing, glue, scissors, felt pen, straight pins. Optional—stapler and staples, hot-glue gun. For each student—one white cotton work glove, small note pad, pencil, small plastic curtain ring.

Preparation: Cut elastic into 6-inch (15-cm) lengths—one for each student. Cut a 16-inch (40-cm) length of yarn for each student.

Instruct each student in the following procedures:

- Write a lesson-related word ("Peace") on fingers of glove (sketch a).
- Fill glove with stuffing, then glue bottom of glove together.
- Glue ends of elastic to glove (sketch b). Straight pins may be used to hold elastic in place until glue dries.

(Optional—you may wrap the elastic around the glove and staple it together in the back.)

- Securely tie one end of yarn to index finger of glove and make a bow.
- Tie other end of yarn to pencil and glue in place.
- Make hanger by gluing curtain ring to back of glove (sketch c). (A hot-glue gun works best.)
- When glue dries on ends of elastic, remove pins and insert note pad (sketch d).

Conversation Suggestions: **How can our hands be used to make peace?** (A friendly pat, holding hands, shaking hands, using hands to help someone or to write a cheerful note.) **When you hang up your Memo Holder it will remind you that *the fruit of the Spirit is peace.***

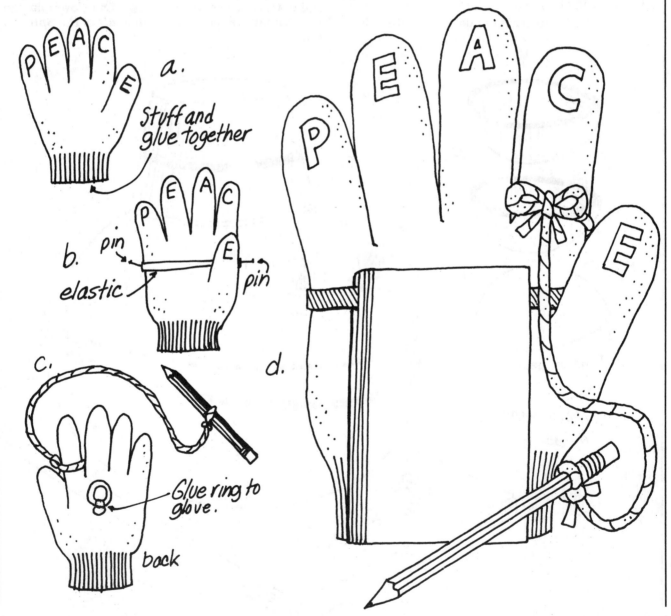

a. stuff and glue together

b. pin — elastic — pin

c. Glue ring to glove. back

d.

Patience Planter

Materials: Can of enamel spray paint, magazines containing pictures of flowers and plants, glue, potting soil, flower seeds, scissors, newspaper. For each student—empty ½ gallon cardboard milk container.

Preparation: Two days before students make this craft, rinse and dry milk cartons thoroughly. Cut cartons in half—to a 5½-inch (13.75-cm) height. Spray-paint cartons and allow to dry at least 24 hours. Cover student's work area with newspaper.

Instruct each student in the following procedures:

• Cut a zigzag design along the top edge of the carton (sketch a).

• Cut pictures of flowers and plants from magazine and glue to sides of carton.

• Fill cartons with potting soil.

• Plant 4 or 5 seeds (sketch b). Water lightly.

Enrichment Idea: Child may letter on a 2×3-inch (5.0×7.5-cm) piece of construction paper *Be patient like a farmer who waits for his harvest to ripen* (see James 5:7).

Conversation Suggestions: **When is a time that it is hard for you to wait? Have you ever planted a seed and wanted it to hurry up and grow? When God created the world, He planned for things to take time to grow and be strong. People take time to grow, too. Do you sometimes wish you could grow up fast? At home you might watch your planter. You will probably wish the seeds would hurry up and grow. Let your planter be a reminder that growing takes time. And that God wants us to have patience, and grow the way He has planned.**

Kindness Flower

Materials: Felt squares, glue, pencils, scissors, newspaper, felt pen. For each student—four 18-inch (45-cm) medium floral wires, one 1½-inch (3.75-cm) pom-pom.

Preparation: Cut felt into 3×4-inch (7.5×10-cm) rectangles—eight for each student. Cover work area with newspaper.

Instruct each student in the following procedures:

• Form a loop at the end of each wire and twist to close loop. (Leave half of wire remaining for stem (sketch a).

• Lay loop on top of felt square.

• Draw a line of glue along loop of wire (sketch b).

• Press another piece of felt over the wire loop. Let dry.

• Repeat process to make three more petals.

• Trim off excess felt from around loop, approximately ⅛ inch from wire.

• Twist the four petals together to form a flower (sketch c).

• Glue a pom-pom to center of flower.

Enrichment Idea: Student letters, "Be ye kind" (see Eph. 4:32.) on the flower—one word on each petal.

Conversation suggestions: **How can you show kindness?** (Show others that you care for them, act in a friendly and helpful way.) **Can you think of some ways to be kind to your family?** Encourage students to think of someone to give their Kindness Flowers to—maybe a person they have a hard time being kind to.

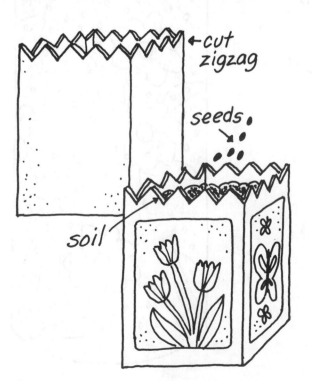

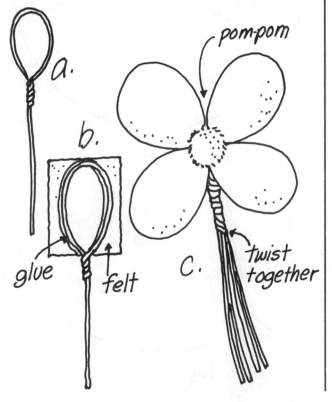

Goodness Light

Materials: Two-ply paper napkins with designs, 3 × 24-inch (7.5 × 60-cm) cylindrical Styrofoam pieces, glue, glitter, felt scraps, scissors, craft knife, pencils, yellow tagboard, felt pen, small containers, paintbrushes, newspapers, damp cloths for cleanup. Optional—large candles may be used in place of Styrofoam.

Preparation: Cover work area with newspaper. Cut Styrofoam into 6-inch lengths—one for each student. Separate plies of napkins. Use only top, printed plies. Cut napkins to fit around Styrofoam cylinders. Make several circle and flame patterns for students to trace. Dilute glue with water and pour into small containers.

Instruct each student in the following procedures:

- Use paintbrush to apply glue to sides of Styrofoam (not on top or bottom).
- Wrap napkin around candle (sketch a).
- Apply a coat of glue over the napkin.
- Sprinkle glitter onto napkin while glue is still wet.
- Let dry. Design will appear when glue has dried.
- Trace circle pattern onto felt and cut out.
- Glue felt circle to top of candle.
- Cut a slit through middle of felt circle into Styrofoam.
- Trace flame pattern onto cardboard and cut out.
- Letter "Let your goodness shine" in the middle of the flame.
- Insert a small amount of glue and then "flame" into slit in top of candle.

Conversation Suggestions: **How can you let your goodness shine? Is it always easy to do what you know is right and good? Why should you do what is good?** (To show love for God. Goodness pleases Him.) **When you love someone, you want to please that person by doing what is good. What are some good things you could do?**

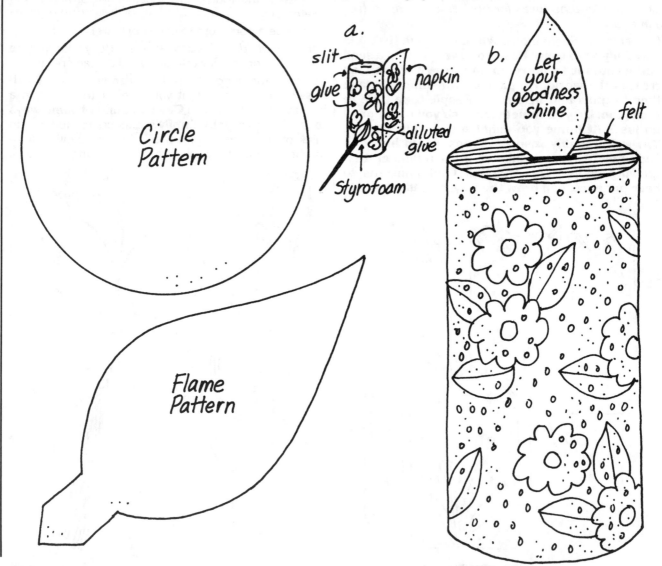

Circle Pattern

Flame Pattern

a.

slit

glue

napkin

diluted glue

Styrofoam

b.

Let your goodness shine

felt

Prayer Reminder

Materials: Colored tagboard, felt tip pens, tacky glue, scissors, construction paper, acrylic paint, paintbrushes, 3×5-inch (7.5×12.5-cm) index cards. For each student—one plastic detergent bottle.

Preparation: Cut bottles in half (sketch a). Rinse and dry bottom section of bottles. Cut construction paper into small rectangles.

Instruct each student in the following procedures:

• Paint bottle.

• Trace both hands onto tagboard. Cut out handprints.

• Draw fingers on hand prints (sketch b).

• Glue hands to opposite sides of bottle.

• Print "I will be faithful to pray for others" on rectangular piece of construction paper.

• Glue paper to bottle, overlapping bottom of hand.

• Write names of people to pray for on index cards.

• Place cards in container (sketch c).

Conversation Suggestions: **Can you think of a person who you can pray for? What might you say in your prayer? Why should you pray for other people? God loves us and listens to all our prayers. The Bible says that it's good for us to pray every day—to be faithful in remembering to talk to God.**

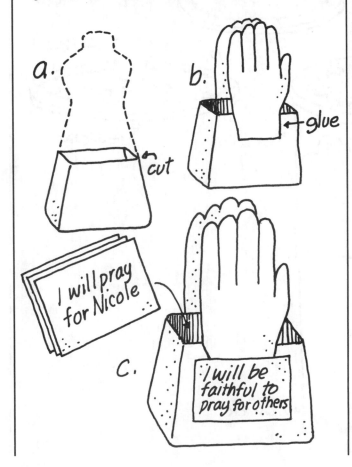

Snow Paperweight

Materials: Moth flakes (if not available—crush moth balls into flakes), teaspoon, water, felt scraps, pencils, scissors, sheets of paper, waterproof glue, paper towels. For each student—a 2-ounce instant coffee (or similar) jar with lid, small ceramic or plastic figure to fit inside jar.

NOTE: Please use caution when working with moth flakes. They may be harmful if ingested or allowed to come into contact with skin.

Instruct each student in the following procedures:

• Glue figure to inside of lid. Let dry thoroughly (sketch a).

• Fill jar with water to ½ inch (1.25-cm) below rim.

• With teacher's help, spoon two teaspoons of moth flakes into water.

• Screw lid on jar. Make sure water level does not go over side of jar. (If it does, remove lid, drain a little water and thoroughly dry rim of jar and lid with paper towels.)

• After you have checked water level, remove lid. Put glue around inside edge of lid. Screw lid onto jar as tightly as possible. Let dry.

• Cut a piece of felt to fit around edge of lid. Glue in place (sketch b).

• Cut a circle of felt to fit on top of jar lid. Glue in place.

Enrichment Idea: On a strip of paper print, "Be gentle" and glue it to bottom of jar. Let dry.

Conversation Suggestions: **Have you ever seen snow falling? How does it make you feel to watch it fall? Watching snow fall makes me think of gentleness. What does it mean for a person to be gentle?**

Cookie Can

Materials: Light-colored spray paint, felt squares, cookie cutters, pencils, sharp-pointed scissors, glue, rickrack, felt pen. Optional—construction paper. For each student—1 lb. coffee can with plastic lid, drawer knob with screw.

Preparation: Spray the outside of cans with paint. (You can stuff cans with newspaper to keep paint from getting on the insides.) Let dry completely—at least 24 hours. Cut rickrack in 13-inch (32.5-cm) lengths—two for each student.

Instruct each student in the following procedures:

• Trace cookie cutters onto felt. Cut out three or four shapes.

• Glue shapes onto can.

• Trace lid onto felt. Cut out.

• Glue felt circle to the lid. Let glue dry for a few minutes.

• Glue one piece of rickrack around edge of felt circle (sketch a).

• Use scissors to poke a small hole in middle of lid.

• Insert screw on underside of lid. Tighten knob onto screw (sketch b).

• With a felt pen write "Cookies" on the lid.

• Glue remaining piece of rickrack around bottom edge of can. Let dry.

Enrichment idea: Letter "The fruit of the Spirit is self-control" on a small piece of construction paper. Glue to can.

Conversation Suggestions: **Do you like cookies? Would it be good for your body if you ate ten cookies for a snack? When you WANT to eat ten cookies but you know you shouldn't so you only take two, you are using self-control. Self-control means you are in control of your mind and body. What are some things we need to control?** (Eating too much junk food, talking during class, watching too much TV, etc.)

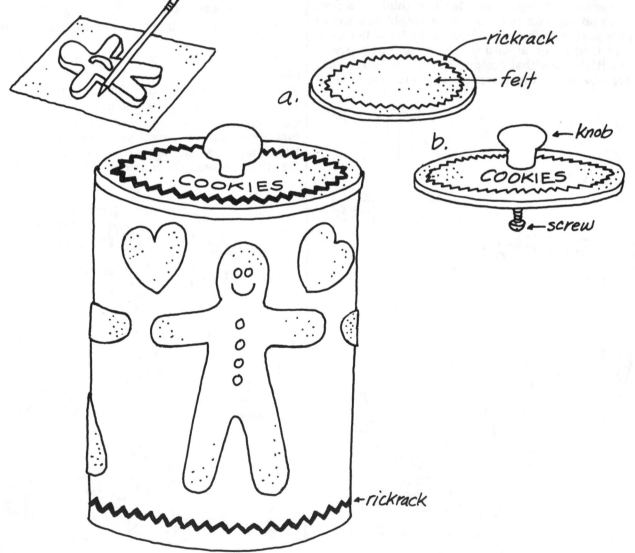

Shadow Box

Materials: Various colors of construction paper, scissors, string, pencils, glue, tape, felt tip pens. Optional—colored cellophane paper. For each student—a shoe box.

Instruct each student in the following procedures:

- Trace the four sides and back of shoe box onto construction paper. Cut out and glue paper inside shoe box to cover interior sides and bottom (sketch a).
- Cut creation scenes out of construction paper (undersea, planets, birds, etc.).
- Use string and tape to hang cut-outs inside box (sketch b).
- Make foreground by cutting construction paper into desired shapes (e.g., bushes, rocks, animals, flowers, etc.). Fold bottom of cut-out toward back and tape to bottom of box. Students may also want to cut out blue construction paper ponds or streams to tape to the "ground" (sketch c).

Enrichment Idea: Cut a piece of cellophane that will cover front of box and will overlap 1 inch on all sides. Tape to box. On piece of paper print, "God created the (planets, birds, etc.)." Tape to cellophane on front of box.

Conversation Suggestions: **There are so many beautiful things that God created. What things would you like to show in your Shadow Box? God created the world then gave it to people to take care of. Have people taken good care of the earth? What things can you do to care for God's creation?**

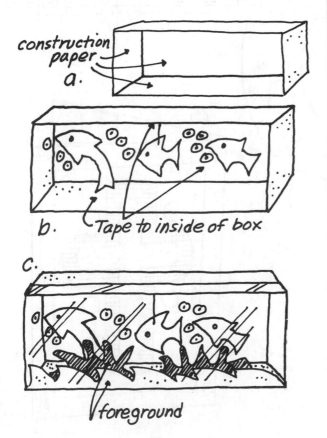

Tile Planter

Materials: Wrapping paper with pictures of flowers or animals (white background works best), caulking material, glue, scissors, pencils, clear acrylic spray. For each student—five 4×4-inch (10×10-cm) white ceramic tiles. Optional—potting soil, flower seeds, small pebbles or charcoal.

Instruct each student in the following procedures:

- Cut out small pictures from wrapping paper.
- Glue pictures to four of the tiles. Let dry.
- Using fifth tile as the base, glue tiles together to form a cube. Seal edges with caulking (see sketch). Let dry.
- Spray planter with clear acrylic paint.

Enrichment Idea: When planter is completely dry, have students line bottom with charcoal or pebbles, then fill with soil and plant seeds. Warn students about overwatering as there is no drain hole.

Conversation Suggestions: **When your planter has dried completely, you can fill it with soil and plant seeds in it. What kind of seeds will you plant? What types of plants grow quickly?** (Grass, radishes, wildflowers.) **Slowly?** (Oak trees, cactus, etc.) **Have you ever planted a seed and wanted it to grow NOW? Can you make things grow faster than God planned for them to grow? YOU are growing, too. How do you feel about growing? God can help you be more patient when you just can't wait to grow up. He will help patience grow inside of you so you'll become better at waiting for ANYTHING!**

Bible Cover

Materials: Felt, rulers, pencils, scissors, glue.

Preparation: (Note: The following measurements will fit standard-sized Bibles. Adjust size to fit students' Bibles if necessary.) Cut felt into 9 × 13-inch (22.5 × 32.5-cm) covers—one for each student. Cut additional felt into 3 × 9-inch (7.5 × 22.5-cm) rectangles—two for each student.

Instruct each student in the following procedures:

• Plan design for cover. It should be simple enough to be cut from felt.

• Cut felt scraps into desired shapes for cover design (sketch a).

• Draw a line of glue on two short edges and one long edge of the two felt rectangles. Glue each rectangle to shorter edge of felt cover to form pockets (sketch b). Be sure to leave inside edges unglued.

• Fold cover in half with pockets on the inside. Use felt shapes to create design on front cover and glue in place (sketch c).

• Let glue dry for a few minutes, then put cover on Bible.

Enrichment Idea: Have students measure and cut their own felt pieces to fit Bibles. Each student will need to cut pieces that are ½-inch (1.25-cm) larger than his or her Bible on each side.

Conversation Suggestions: **Why is your Bible special to you? What important truths have you learned from reading your Bible? When you read the Bible, God is communicating with you. He is telling you how much He loves you and how you can show love to others. This cover will help protect your Bible and show others that the Word of God is special to you.**

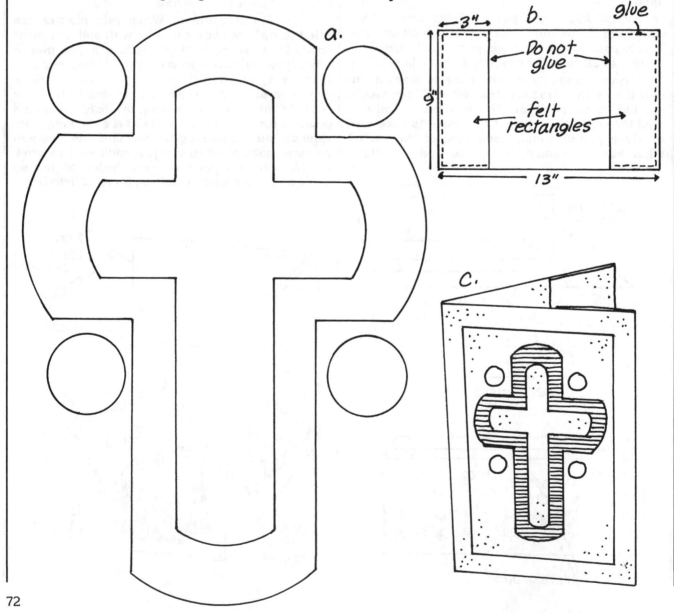

Joyful Clown

Materials: Lightweight cardboard or tagboard, tracing or tissue paper, yarn, scissors, felt pens, tacky glue, scraps of felt, clear acrylic spray, stapler, construction paper, acrylic paints, small paintbrushes. For each student—one egg-shaped pantyhose container and one 5 oz. cup.

Preparation: Cut yarn into 4-inch (10-cm) lengths—about twenty for each student. Cut construction paper into 1½ × 6-inch (3.75 × 15-cm) pieces—one for each student. To make sturdy patterns, trace bow tie pattern onto tracing paper, then cut out and trace onto cardboard. Cut one cardboard pattern for every two or three students.

Instruct each student in the following procedures:
- Glue halves of egg-shaped container together.
- Paint clown face on egg (sketch a). Let dry.
- Paint cup.
- Spray egg with acrylic spray to "set" paint.
- To make a base for the egg, staple ends of construction paper rectangle together.
- Place a line of glue along top rim of base and insert egg (sketch b). Let dry.
- Glue yarn pieces to top of egg for clown's hair.
- Trace bow tie pattern onto felt. Cut out.
- Glue bow tie to base at clown's "neck."
- Glue cup to top of clown's head for hat (sketch c).

Conversation Suggestions: **Have you ever seen a clown in a circus? How did the clown make people laugh? Funny tricks and silliness make us laugh and feel happy, but is that kind of happiness the same thing as joy? How is the happiness we feel when laughing at a clown different from joy? Happy feelings can go away or change quickly into other kinds of feelings—sometimes sadness, frustration, anger. The kind of joy the Bible talks about is felt inside, too, but it doesn't change. Joy is always believing that God loves you and is taking care of you, no matter how happy or sad you feel.**

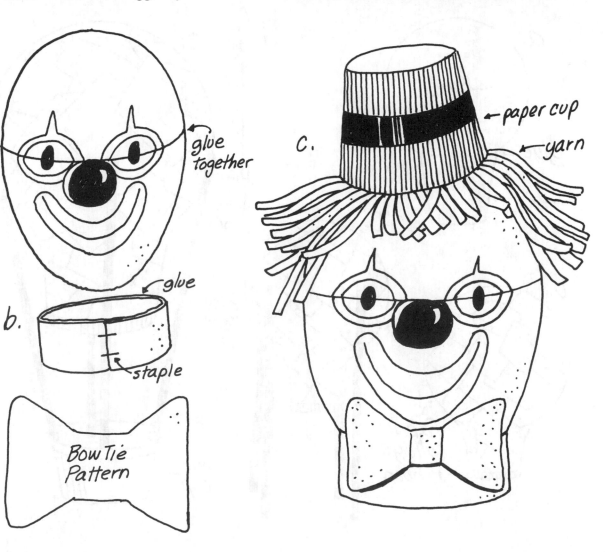

a.

glue together

b. glue

staple

Bow Tie Pattern

c. paper cup

yarn

Hot Air Balloon

Materials: Fabric or felt scraps, scissors, tacky glue, narrow ribbon, straight pins, fishing line, stapler. For each student—one 4-inch (10-cm) Styrofoam ball, one 3-oz. paper cup, one nut cup.

Preparation: Cut ribbon into one 8-inch (20-cm) and four 10-inch (25-cm) lengths for each student.

Instruct each student in the following procedures:

• Glue rim of 3-oz. cup to Styrofoam ball (sketch a). Let dry.

• Cut fabric or felt scraps into small squares.

• Glue scraps on ball and cup to cover "balloon."

• Glue the shortest length of ribbon around base of balloon (sketch b).

• Glue one end of each of the other four ribbon lengths to balloon (sketch c). Insert pins into ball to hold ribbon in place until glue dries.

• Tie one end of fishing line to head of straight pin (sketch d).

• To be able to hang the balloon, make a loop on the other end of line.

• Put glue on pin and insert into top of balloon.

• Glue or staple loose ends of ribbon to the nut cup (sketch e).

Enrichment Idea: Fill the nut cups with peanuts, raisins, banana chips, etc.

Conversation Suggestions: **How do you think it would feel to float high above the ground in a hot air balloon? What might you see? Hear? Floating slowly through the air would be a quiet and peaceful experience. What does peace mean to you?** (It is not fighting; solving problems without violence.) **God wants us all to solve our problems peacefully. Your balloons can be reminders of the peace God wants each of us to have.**

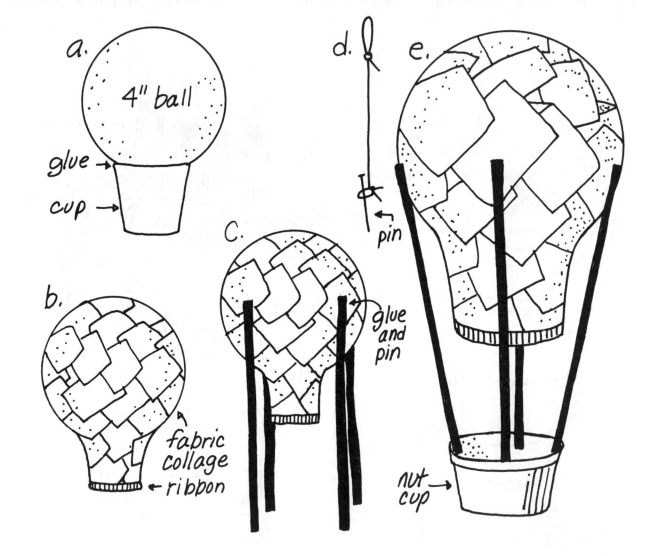

a. 4" ball
glue →
cup →

b. fabric collage ← ribbon

c. glue and pin

d. 📌 pin

e. nut → cup

Bird House

Materials: Rolls of colorful self-adhesive paper, sharp-pointed scissors, masking tape, glue. For each student—one shoe box, one wire coat hanger. Optional—birdseed, small plastic bags, craft knife.

Preparation: Cut self-adhesive paper into 2-foot (.6-m) lengths—one for each student.

Instruct each student in the following procedures:

- Bend hanger (sketch a).
- Cut a hole in the center of one end of the shoe box. (If students find cutting with scissors difficult, you may help them use craft knife to CAREFULLY cut window.)
- Cut a hole in side of box near one end. Repeat procedure on other side of box (sketch b).
- Insert top of hanger in hole in end of box and sides of the hanger in side holes (sketch c). (The hanger inside the box is a perch for the bird.)

- Cut three sides of a door near the bottom of the box lid. Bend door hinge down, fold back and glue to make "porch" (sketch d).
- Cut a round window in box lid.
- Place lid on box with door at the bottom. Tape lid to box (sketch e).
- Cover bird house with self-adhesive paper. Use scissors to cut out paper that covers holes.

Enrichment Idea: Give each student a plastic bag containing birdseed to take home.

Conversation Suggestions: **What kinds of birds do you see near your house? Where would be a good place to hang your bird house? Why do you think a bird might like a house? What do birds like to eat? You might put some birdseed inside the house and watch the birds come and eat the seeds. Feeding and taking care of the creatures God made is a way to show kindness.**

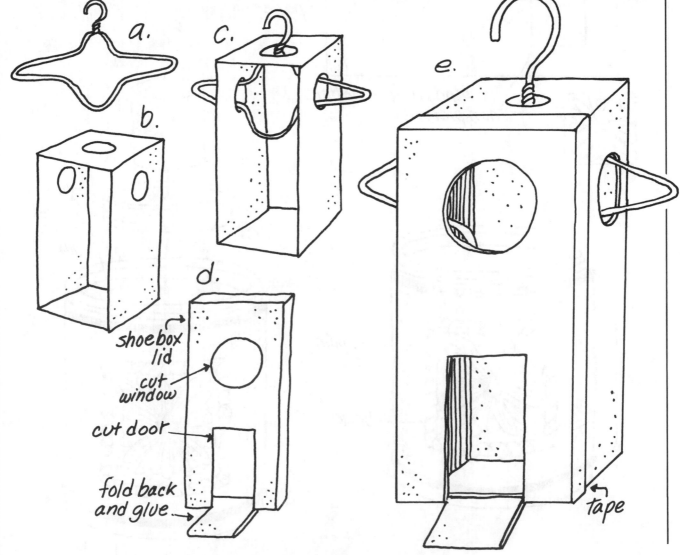

a.

b.

c.

d. shoebox lid

cut window

cut door

fold back and glue

e.

tape

Goodness Glow Jar

Materials: Magazines, decorative braid, gold cording, solid color wrapping paper, scissors, tacky glue, pencils. For each student—one votive candle, one wide mouth pint jar, one small metal or plastic jar lid. (A wide mouth jar must be used for adequate air circulation so the candle will burn steadily and not smoke.)

Instruct each student in the following procedures:

- Cut a small, colorful picture from a magazine.
- Cut a piece of wrapping paper to cover the jar.
- Cut a "window" in the wrapping paper to frame the magazine picture. Window should be ¼ inch (.60 cm) smaller on all sides than picture (sketch a).
- Center picture vertically on jar and glue in place.
- Glue wrapping paper around jar, framing picture.
- Cut braid to fit around picture and glue in place.
- Cut cord to fit around top and bottom of jar and glue in place (sketch b).
- Glue small jar lid (rim side up) to inside bottom of jar (sketch c).
- Place votive candle inside jar lid.

Conversation Suggestions: **When you light your candle in a dark room, what will happen? The darkness will be overpowered by the light. Light is more powerful than darkness. The Bible says to "let your light shine." One way to let our lights shine is to show God's love and goodness to those around us. What are some ways you can let your light shine?**

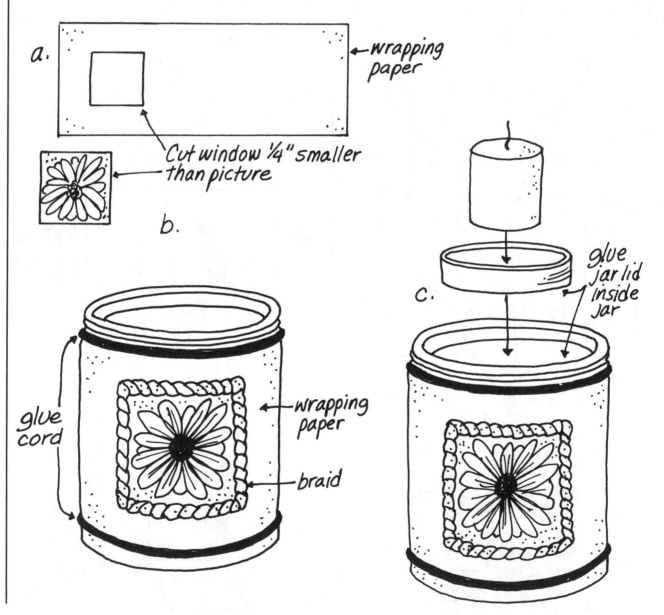

a. wrapping paper

Cut window ¼" smaller than picture

b.

glue cord

wrapping paper

braid

c. glue jar lid inside jar

Prayer Calendar

Materials: Scissors, 9 × 12-inch (22.5 × 30-cm) sheets of construction paper, scissors, yarn, glue, felt tip pens, rulers, pictures from old calendars, pictures from used greeting cards or Bible pictures from old Sunday School materials, hole punch; photocopies of medium-sized calendar pages (for months remaining in calendar year)—one set for each student.

Instruct each student in the following procedures:

• Glue photocopied calendar pages to the bottom halves of construction paper sheets—one page to each sheet (sketch a).

• Glue Bible story picture or greeting card to the top half of each paper, above the calendar.

• On each page of the calendar print, "I will remember to pray for" and draw a blank line on which student may write names of people to pray for (sketch a).

• Glue a large picture (from old calendar) on a sheet of construction paper for cover page and write, "I will be faithful to pray for others."

• Punch two holes near the top edge of each page, lining holes up to make sure they match.

• Put the pages of the calendar in order.

• Cut a 24-inch (60-cm) piece of yarn and thread it through the holes. Tie ends of yarn together (sketch b). Be sure the yarn is loose enough so the pages can be turned easily.

Conversation Suggestions: **Can you think of someone you know who has a special need right now—maybe someone who is hurt or lonely or unhappy? What could you do to help that person? One way to help people is to remember to pray for them. Think of a person right now who you can pray for and write that person's name on the first month of your calendar. Every month you can write different names on your calendar. It will help you remember to be faithful in prayer and God will increase your willingness to help that person.**

a. construction paper

I will remember to pray for _____

June

SUN	MON	TUES	WED	THURS	FRI	SAT

b. I will be faithful to pray for others.

Pinecone Rabbit

Materials: Cotton balls, pencils, scissors, tracing or tissue paper, glue, white lightweight cardboard, pink and blue felt scraps, pink or black chenille wire, black felt tip pen, pieces of Styrofoam or heavy cardboard, construction paper. For each student—one open pinecone, two medium wiggle eyes.

Preparation: To make sturdy ear and feet patterns, trace patterns onto tracing paper, then cut out and trace onto cardboard. Cut one cardboard pattern for every two or three students.

Instruct each student in the following procedures:

• Pull apart cotton balls and insert into the pine cone, filling the spaces to make pinecone look "fluffy."

• To make ears, trace ear pattern twice onto cardboard and twice onto pink felt. Cut out.

• Glue felt ears to cardboard ears (sketch a).

• With felt tip pen, draw a line on each ear (sketch b).

• Place glue along the bottom of each ear and push into pinecone.

• Cut two small circles (blue) and one small triangle (pink) out of felt for eyes and nose.

• Glue eyes and nose onto rabbit.

• Glue wiggle eyes onto felt eyes.

• Cut chenille wire into 6 pieces. Place glue on the end of each wire and push into pinecone for whiskers (sketch c).

• Trace feet pattern onto white cardboard and cut out.

• Glue bottom of pinecone rabbit to cardboard feet.

• To make a base, glue finished rabbit to a piece of Styrofoam or circle of heavy cardboard.

Enrichment Idea: Print "Be humble and gentle" on a small piece of paper. Glue onto base.

Conversation Suggestions: **What does gentleness mean to you? What is the opposite of gentleness? Can you think of some times you need to be especially gentle? You can learn to be gentle with your actions, your words and your attitude. Harsh actions and words can hurt; gentle actions and words can help. What does it mean to have a gentle attitude?** (Being willing to listen and learn.) **The rabbit you're making can help you remember what the Bible teaches about gentleness.**

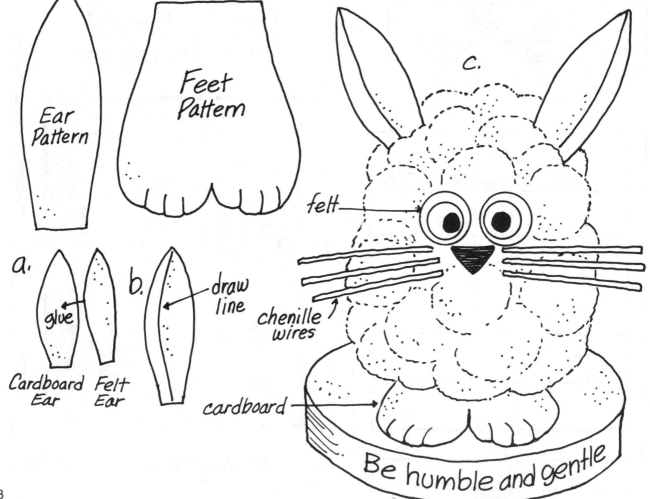

"Fruit of the Spirit" Tree

Materials: Bibles, tagboard, heavy cardboard, felt (pink, red, green and brown), pencils, scissors, ¾-inch (1.9-cm) Velcro (available by the yard in fabric stores), glue, construction paper, felt tip pen. For each student—one 9 × 12-inch (22.5 × 30-cm) piece of blue felt.

Preparation: Use tagboard to make apple and blossom patterns—one for every three or four students. Cut brown felt into 3 × 6-inch (7.5 × 15.-cm) pieces—one for each student. Cut green felt into 7 × 8-inch (17.5 × 20-cm) pieces—one for each student. Cut heavy cardboard into 9 × 12-inch (22.5 × 30-cm) pieces—one for each student. Cut Velcro strip into ¼-inch (.65-cm) pieces—five for each student.

Instruct each student in the following procedures:
- Glue blue felt to cardboard.
- Cut tree top shape from piece of green felt.
- Cut tree trunk shape from piece of brown felt.
- Glue tree top and trunk to blue felt.
- Trace blossom pattern onto pink felt five times. Cut out.
- Trace apple pattern onto red felt five times. Cut out.
- Glue blossoms to tree top.

- Take the Velcro pieces apart. Glue each rough piece above a blossom on the tree (sketch a).
- Glue each fuzzy piece of Velcro to a felt apple (sketch b).
- Look up Galatians 5:22,23 in Bible and choose five qualities of the Fruit of the Spirit. Print the words ("Kindness," "Peace," "Faithfulness," "Joy," etc.) on a piece of paper. Cut each word out and glue to the side of the apple without Velcro. Let dry.
- On a piece of paper print a short phrase that tells about the meaning of each word glued to an apple. (E.g., "help others," "do good for others," "be honest," "thank God in song," "don't fight," etc.). Cut each phrase out and glue one on each blossom.
- Use Velcro tabs to fasten each apple over the corresponding blossom.

Conversation Suggestions: **God wants the fruit of the Spirit to grow in each of your lives. This tree shows some of the parts of the fruit of the Spirit. What does kindness mean to you? Tell me what peace is. How do you show faithfulness? What is joy? How do you learn to control yourself?** (As discussion continues, students may be encouraged to think of short phrases to write for each blossom.)

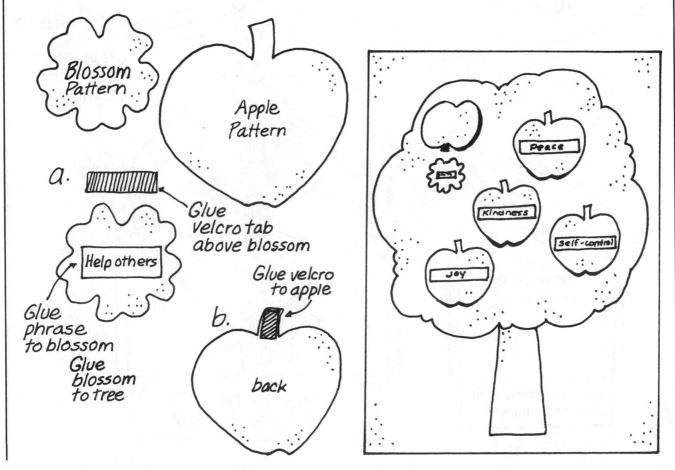

Sun Catcher

Materials: Crepe paper (green, yellow and orange), tagboard or heavy paper, ribbon, glue, scissors, felt pens, clear plastic wrap. For each student—four ice cream or craft sticks, a ½-inch (1.25-cm) yellow pom-pom, two chenille wires.

Preparation: From tagboard cut a 1 × 5-inch (2.5 × 12.5-cm) strip—one for each student. Cut plastic wrap into 4½-inch (11.25-cm) squares—one for each student.

Instruct each student in the following procedures:

- Cut 28 green leaves, 8 yellow petals and 4 orange petals from crepe paper (sketch a).
- Glue sticks together to form a square (sketch b).
- Glue clear plastic wrap to top of sticks. Let dry.
- Letter the words "Let the Goodness of the Lord Shine Through" (or other lesson-related phrase) on the tagboard strip.
- Bend chenille wire the shape of three sides of a square. Glue tagboard to bottom portion of wire and let dry (sketch c).

- Glue chenille wire to craft stick square (sketch d).
- Glue the leaves to the craft sticks. Then arrange and glue the petals in center of plastic square to make a flower.
- Glue the pom-pom in the middle of the flower.
- Cut a length of ribbon and glue it to top of square. Loop at end to make hanger.

Conversation Suggestions: **Listen to this Bible verse, then tell us what God has made. Read *And God made the two great lights: the greater light to govern the day, and the lesser light to govern the night. He made the stars also.* (see Genesis 1:16). What is the greater light? The lesser light? Why do we need the sun? The moon? Could we ever fly to the sun? Why not? God has placed the sun just the right distance from our earth. When we see the sun through our Sun Catcher, we can remember God's creation.**

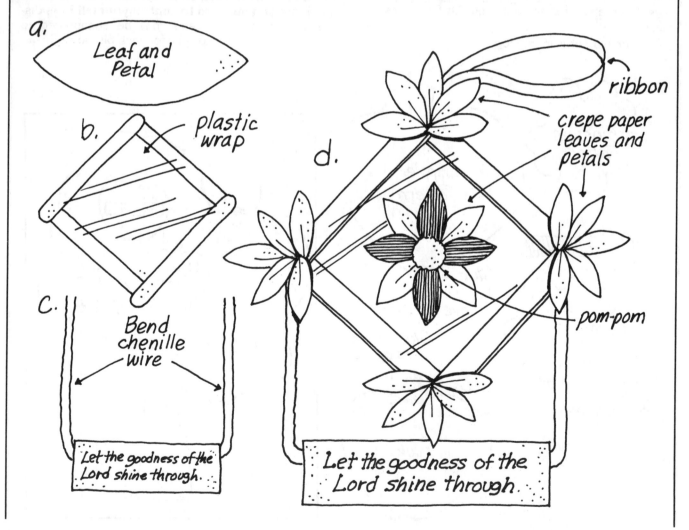

a. Leaf and Petal

b. plastic wrap

c. Bend chenille wire

Let the goodness of the Lord shine through.

d. ribbon

crepe paper leaves and petals

pom-pom

Let the goodness of the Lord shine through.

Critters

Materials: Chenille wires, small pom-poms, felt scraps, scissors, glue. For each student—one spring-type clothespin, one set of wiggle eyes.

Preparation: Cut chenille wires in half. Remove springs from clothespins. (Wooden clothespin pieces may be used in "Clothespin Cross" craft.)

Instruct each student in the following procedures:

- Push two chenille wires through center of spring (sketch a).
- Bend wires to form legs and feet (sketch b).
- Glue pom-poms to one end of spring for face.
- Add felt tail and wiggle eyes.

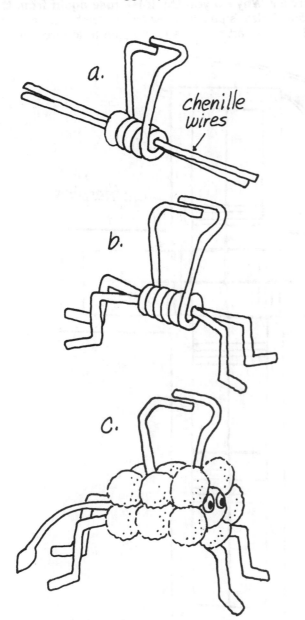

Napkin Rings

Materials: Paper towel tubes, craft sticks, several colors of poster paint, paintbrushes, felt pens, package of colorful paper napkins. For each student—a lunch-size paper bag.

Preparation: Cut paper towel tube into 1½-inch (3.75-cm) sections—one for each member of each student's family (sketch a).

Instruct each student in the following procedures:

- Paint outside and edges of napkin rings.
- After paint dries, use felt pen to letter "Thank You, God" on each napkin ring.
- Fold napkins as shown in sketch b.
- Place a napkin in each ring (sketch c).
- Put napkin rings and napkins in paper bag to carry home.

Conversation Suggestions: **How do you think God feels when we remember to thank Him for our food? Why do you think God is pleased? Why do you think God keeps helping us have the things we need?** (God loves us very much.) **Your napkin rings will help you and your family remember to thank God for your food.** Volunteers may share their family's mealtime prayer with the group.

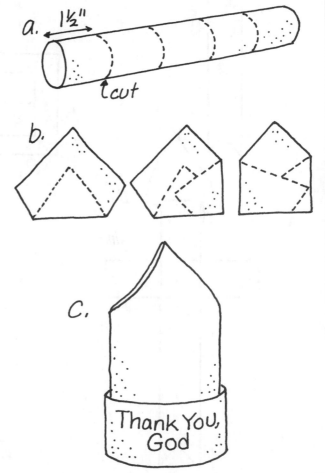

Clothespin Cross

Materials: Gold metallic thread, tacky glue, 1½-inch (3.75-cm) ribbon. For each student—five spring-type clothespins.

Preparation: Remove springs from clothespins. Cut ribbon into 15-inch (37.5-cm) and 9-inch (22.5-cm) lengths—one of each for each student. Cut metallic thread into 4-inch (10-cm) lengths—one for each student.

Instruct each student in the following procedures:

• Fold 1 inch (2.5 cm) of longer piece of ribbon back and crease it.

• Tie ends of a 4-inch (10-cm) length of metallic thread together.

• Place tied metallic thread inside the fold and glue folded portion to back of ribbon to form hanger (sketch a).

• Fold shorter piece of ribbon in half to find midpoint.

• Glue center of shorter ribbon across longer ribbon about 5 inches (12.5 cm) from top, forming a cross (sketch b).

• Glue clothespin pieces onto horizontal bar of ribbon two pieces wide, flat side down. Repeat procedure on vertical bar of ribbon (sketch c).

Conversation Suggestions: Ask simple questions to help students recall the events of Jesus' death and resurrection. **Why do you think Jesus died on the cross? Why do you think He rose again from the dead?** Help students know Jesus' death and resurrection were part of God's loving plan to forgive our sins and give us eternal life.

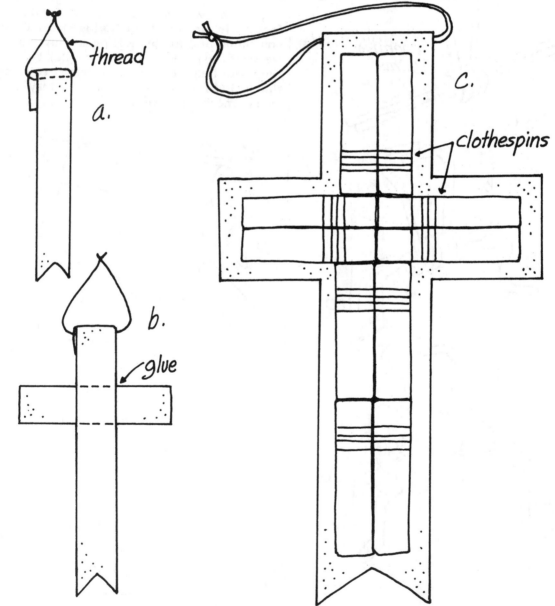

thread

a.

b.

glue

c.

clothespins

Craft Stick Napkin Holder

Materials: Tacky glue, flat toothpicks, lightweight poster board, felt pens, newsprint or butcher paper. For each student—sixteen ice cream or craft sticks.

Preparation: Cover work area with newsprint. Cut poster board into triangles with equal sides of 4 inches (10 cm)—two for each student.

Instruct each student in the following procedures:

• Glue three craft sticks together to form a triangle, overlapping ends of each stick (sketch a). Set aside and allow to dry. (Each student should make two triangles).

• Using toothpicks, apply glue to the narrow edge of five craft sticks. Glue the sticks together (sketch b).

• Glue five more sticks on top of first five to make a sturdy base.

• Letter an appropriate Bible verse or prayer on one of the poster board triangles and decorate. Leave ½-inch (1.25-cm) margin around outside edge of triangle.

• Glue one poster board triangle to the back of each craft stick triangle (sketch c). Let dry.

• Stand triangles on either side of base and glue.

• Brace sides with boxes or books while drying.

Conversation Suggestions: **What does the verse on your holder say? What can you do to obey this verse at mealtimes?**

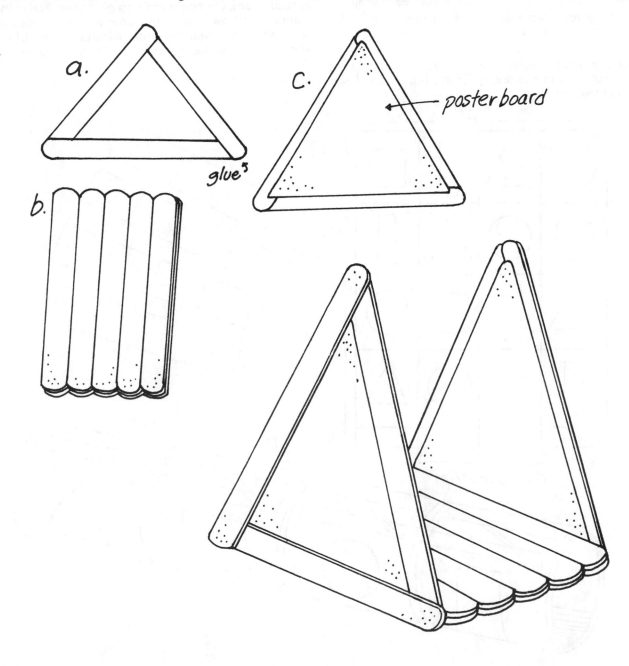

a.

glue³

b.

c.

— posterboard

Share-a-Toy
(Matching Game)

Materials: Felt pens, 8 × 10-inch (20 × 25-cm) sheets of light-colored construction paper, scissors, tape, rulers. For each student—a potato chip or tennis ball can.

Preparation: Arrange with your Kindergarten Department leader for an appropriate time when your group can demonstrate and give Matching Games to kindergartners.

Instruct each student in the following procedures:

• Draw grid (shown in sketch a) on sheet of paper. (Sixteen rectangles—2 × 2³⁄₈ inches.)

• Select four shapes to draw (e.g., triangle, square, rectangle, circle) and a different color for each shape.

• Draw and color a different shape in each box in the first column of the grid.

• In the second, third and fourth columns, draw and color the same shapes (each shape maintaining the same color as in the first column), but in a different order (sketch a).

• Cut apart the columns to make four strips.

• Tape the strips around the can, overlapping edges (sketch b). Strips should turn easily.

• Turn the strips until one set of colored shapes is aligned.

Conversation Suggestions: **The boys and girls in our Kindergarten Department will have fun playing with the Matching Games you are making. Our Bible tells us to share what we have with others.** (See Hebrews 13:16.) **When we go into the Kindergarten room, choose a child to give your Matching Game to. Show him or her how to match the colored shapes. Then let your Kindergarten friend show you how he or she has learned to match them.** If there are more kindergartners than there are Matching Games, suggest children take turns.

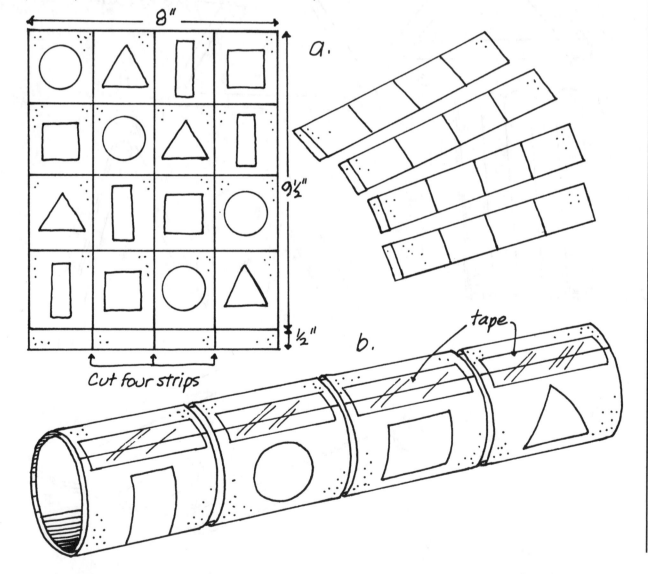

Papier-Maché Gift Egg

(A Two-Day Project)

Materials: Newspaper or newsprint, flour, water, spoons, small containers, glue, masking tape, poster paints and paintbrushes. For each student—one plastic egg-shaped pantyhose container, four pieces of wrapped candy, one Styrofoam cup, a 2 × 3-inch (5 × 7.5-cm) piece of paper (for Bible verse).

Preparation: Tear newspaper into ½-inch (1.25-cm) strips of various lengths. Prepare flour paste by mixing 1 cup flour with ¾ cup water. Add flour to thicken, water to thin as necessary. Paste should have the consistency of wallpaper paste. Spoon paste into containers.

Instruct each student in the following procedures:

Day 1:

• Use masking tape to cover threads that connect egg halves.

• Dip paper strips in paste. Pull the paper between second and third fingers to remove excess paste. Apply strips to egg one at a time, forming several layers. (Do not paper over masking tape.)

• Set egg on Styrofoam cup and allow to dry.

Day 2:

• Decorate dry egg with poster paints. Let dry.

• Remove masking tape from egg threads.

• On paper, letter "Share with others." Place paper and four pieces of candy inside egg.

Conversation Suggestions: **Giving gifts is a way we can show our love. To whom will you give your Gift Egg? How do you think** (your friend) **will feel when he opens the egg? You are obeying what our Bible tells us to do.** *Share with others* (see Hebrews 13:16).

Do not paper over threads

Fruit of the Spirit Basket

Materials: Bright colored tempera or acrylic paints, paintbrushes, black felt pens, chalkboard and chalk or butcher paper and masking tape. For each student— one plastic berry basket, two chenille wires, three medium-sized smooth stones.

Preparation: Wash stones and baskets. On chalkboard or large piece of paper letter the fruit of the Spirit: love, joy, peace, patience, kindness, goodness, faithfulness, gentleness, self-control (see Galatians 5:22,23).

Instruct each student in the following procedures:

• Paint stones on one side. Let dry.

• Make a double handle on basket by twisting chenille wires to two opposite sides of basket. (Handles should be at least 1 inch (2.5 cm) apart for stability.)

• Select three of the fruit of the Spirit from list you have posted. Use felt pen to letter names on stones— one on each stone.

• When dry, turn stones over and paint other side.

• Place stones in basket.

Conversation Suggestions: As students work, point to the list of the fruit of the Spirit you have posted. Say, **These words describe the kind of person God wants to help us to be. Pick out a word. Then tell us how you would show** (love). **For example, I'll choose the word patience. When I have patience, I will wait my turn in traffic or at the market checkout line without getting angry. If someone behind me is in a very big hurry, I'll let that person go in front of me.**

Papier-Maché Puppet
(A Two-Day Project)

Materials: Small round balloons, newsprint or newspaper strips, flour, water, spoons, small containers, poster paints, paintbrushes, fabric, glue, masking tape, needle.

Preparation: Tear strips of newspaper into ½-inch (1.25-cm) strips of various lengths. Prepare flour paste by mixing 1 cup flour with ¾ cup water. Add flour to thicken, water to thin as necessary. Paste should be consistency of wallpaper paste. Spoon paste into containers.

Instruct each student in the following procedures:

Day 1:

• Blow up balloon and tie.

• Wet strips of paper in paste. Pull strips between fingers to remove excess paste. Apply one strip at a time until balloon is covered (sketch a).

• Apply several layers, leaving a 1-inch (2.5-cm) diameter opening around the bottom of the balloon. Let dry overnight.

Day 2:

• Glue down any loose strips.

• Paint over paper mache, making facial features and hair. (Yarn can be used for hair.)

• After paint drys, pop balloon with needle.

• Make binding around opening with masking tape (sketch b). Place two fingers in opening to use as puppet.

Conversation Suggestions: After puppets are complete, say, **Let's use our puppets to play out "The Good Samaritan" Bible story** (see Luke 10:29-37). Or, use another Bible story familiar to your group. Ask questions to help students recall story action. Then students select characters (man, robbers, priest, Levite, good Samaritan, innkeeper) to portray. Guide the action by saying, **Here comes the** (priest). **What is he going to do?** Play out the story a second time, using other students so all have a turn.

a.

b.

masking tape

Clothespin Planter

Materials: Glue, wooden clothespins (not spring-type), acrylic paint, paintbrushes. For each student—one clean, 12½ ounce tuna can, a small potted plant, potting soil.

Preparation: None.

Instruct each student in the following procedures:

- Run a line of glue down the outside of the can. Place a clothespin on the glue, fitting it over the edge of the can (sketch a).
- Repeat process with clothespins until entire can is covered (sketch b).
- Paint the clothespins with acrylic paint. Let dry.
- Place potted plant inside of planter.

Conversation Suggestions: **Think of one of the very best gifts you've ever been given. What was it? Who gave it to you? Why? Was the gift important to you because of who gave it? Why do we give gifts? To whom will you give your planter? Why do you think** (your mom) **will be pleased?** (Because you showed your love for her). **What was God's best gift to us? Why did God send Jesus to us?**

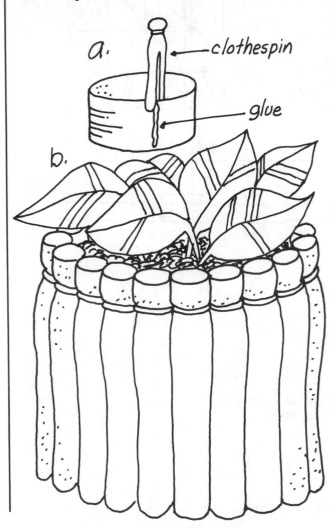

Cloved Fruit Balls

Materials: Apples, oranges, whole cloves, toothpicks, ribbon.

Preparation: None.

Instruct each student in the following procedures:

- Choose a piece of fruit. If fruit has a thick skin, use a toothpick to make holes, then push a clove stud into each hole.
- Cover the entire fruit with cloves, leaving a small space for tying a ribbon around it (see sketch). Tie a loop at top of bow so fruit ball can be hung up.
- Hang fruit ball to dry. When it is completely dry, it is ready to hang in closet.

Conversation Suggestions: **What does the smell of an apple remind you of? The smell of cloves? What things remind you of the good times we've had learning about God's love? Hang your fruit ball in your closet and perhaps when you open your closet door and smell the cloves, you'll remember the good times we've had together.**

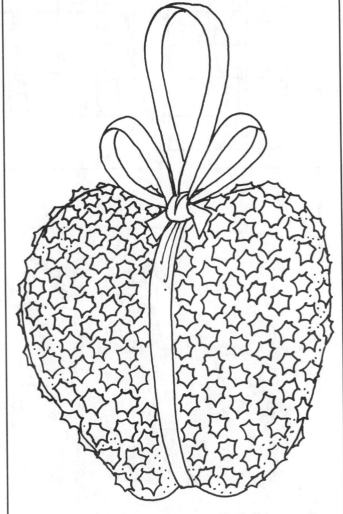

Noah's Two-By-Two Pictures

Materials: Tagboard, straight pins, butcher paper, tacks or masking tape, poster paint in a variety of colors, paintbrushes, scissors, pencils.

Preparation: To make animal patterns, enlarge animal outlines by drawing a grid of one inch (2.5 cm) squares, 4×6-inches (10×15-cm), as shown in sketch a. Draw the animal square by square on the grid. Cut out one of each animal. Cut butcher paper into 14×16-inch (35×40-cm) pieces—one for each student. Tack papers to bulletin board or tape to wall. Optional—for a group project, post a large piece of butcher paper on the wall (or outdoors) and have students make a mural.

Instruct each student in the following procedures:

• Select an animal. Trace animal onto tagboard and cut out.

• Place animal pattern on butcher paper. (Be sure to leave enough room on the paper to repeat the animal outline and draw an ark outline.)

• Fasten pattern securely to butcher paper with several pins.

• Paint around edges of animal pattern with poster paint, extending the paint beyond the pattern.

• Carefully remove pattern. Repeat the animal outline on another area of the paper using a different color paint (sketch b).

• Outline an ark with paint.

Conversation Suggestions: **Why did God tell Noah to build an ark? How do you think Noah felt about what God told him? If you had been Noah, how might you have felt? What kind of problems do you think Noah might have had on the ark? How do you think he solved them?**

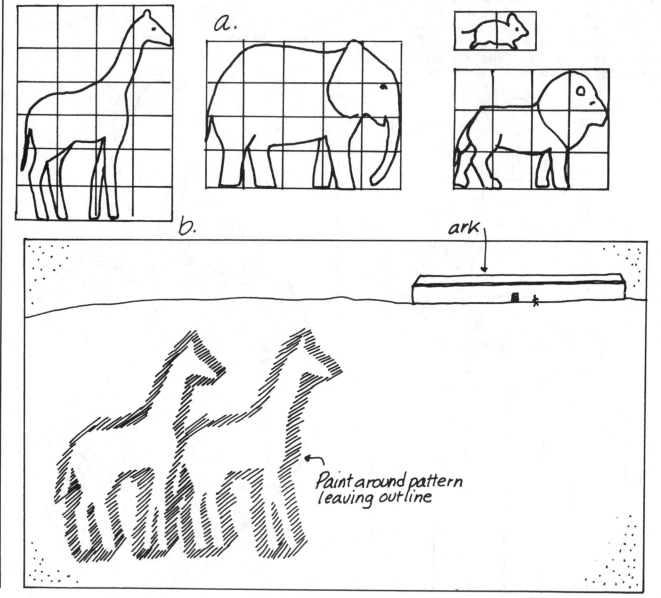

a.

b.

ark

Paint around pattern leaving outline

Snowflakes

Materials: Flour, salt, egg, pastry brush, large and small plastic mixing bowls, small cookie cutters, knives, spoons, narrow ribbon, spray varnish, rolling pins, cookie sheet. You will also need access to an oven.

Preparation: Make dough using two parts flour, one part salt and one part water. Form a ball and knead the dough 7 to 10 minutes until it has a smooth, firm consistancy. Beat egg. Cut ribbon into 8-inch (20-cm) lengths—one for each student.

Instruct each student in the following procedures:

- Roll the dough ¼-inch (.625-cm) thick.
- Cut out large snowflake shape (sketch a).
- Use cookie cutters and knife to cut smaller shapes from the large snowflake.
- Brush finished snowflakes with beaten egg and bake in a 325°F (160°C) oven for ½ hour. Let cool.
- Spray on varnish to seal the surfaces. Let dry.
- Tie a ribbon through one of the holes (sketch b).

Conversation Suggestions: **God makes each snowflake different from every other one. In what ways has God made us different from each other? Like each other? What is good about being different? About being similar? What is one thing all of us who are Christians want to do?** (Love and obey God.)

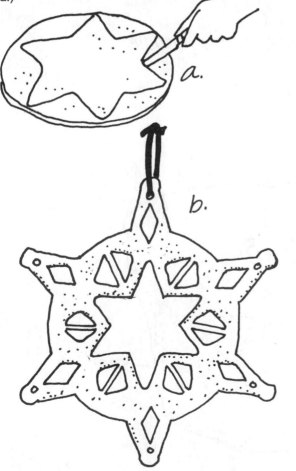

Soap Sculpture (Bas-relief)

(Bas-relief is sculpture using only one side of the block.)

Materials: Pencils, paper, newspaper, knives (table, pocket, kitchen) pointed instruments such as a knitting needle. For each student—a bar of soft soap (such as Ivory).

Preparation: Cover work area with newspapers.

Instruct each student in the following procedures:

- On paper trace around the large side of the soap bar (sketch a).
- Using outline as a frame, sketch design to be carved.
- Place sketch on soap. Use pencil to trace through paper onto soap (sketch b).
- Remove paper. Use knife and other instruments to carve design.
- Cut away the background, so the design is about ¼ inch (.625 cm) higher than the background (sketch c).

Enrichment Idea: Students mix Ivory Snow soap flakes with water and food coloring and mold mixture like clay.

Conversation Suggestions: **Did you know God was the very first sculptor? He was! When God created the world, what things did He sculpt?** (Mountains, glaciers, hills.) **Which ones are smooth? Jagged? Our Bible tells us,** *God formed mountains and made the winds* (see Amos 4:13).

Sand Candles

Materials: Parafin wax and crayons or discarded candles, double boiler or a large tin can in a sauce pan, hot plate or stove, box of sand, water. For each student—one votive candle.

Preparation: Melt wax in double boiler or in a tin can in a sauce pan of water. Add a few crayons for color. Heat the wax to 240°F (121°C) if you want lots of sand to stick to the candle, 200°F (93°C) if you want a small amount of sand to stick. Allow water to boil for a few minutes and then begin to cool before using melted wax.

Instruct each student in the following procedures:

• Moisten sand with water (just until damp, not wet and runny). Pack the sand firmly.

• Hollow out a shape for the candle in the sand.

• Place the votive candle in hole in sand.

• Slowly pour the wax into the hole and fill to the top of the votive candle.

• After wax hardens, dig sand away from candle. Lift it carefully from the box. Brush off loose sand (sketch b).

Conversation Suggestions: **What kind of light do you think Jesus meant when He said, *I have come as light into the world, that everyone who believes in Me may not remain in darkness?* (John 12:46 *NASB*.) When He said, *Let your light shine before men in such a way that they may see your good works, and glorify your Father who is in heaven?* (Matthew 5:16 *NASB*.) What kind of light do you think the Psalmist meant when he said, *Thy word is a lamp to my feet, and a light to my path?* (Psalm 119:105 *NASB*.)**

melted wax

a.

hole dug in sand

votive candle

b.

sand

Relief Map

Materials: Cornstarch, salt, water, spoons, twine, sand, pebbles, straw flowers, twigs, Bible geography books showing biblical lands. For each student—one 8 × 11-inch (20 × 27.5-cm) piece of heavy corrugated cardboard.

Preparation: Make dough by mixing 1 part cornstarch, 3 parts salt and just enough water to make a putty-like consistency. Knead until smooth.

Instruct each student in the following procedures:

• Choose one scene to recreate from his or her favorite Bible story. For example, The Birth of Jesus (Luke 2:1-20); Prodigal Son (Luke 15:11-24); Escape from Egypt (Exodus 14:21,22).

• Cover the surface of the cardboard with dough. Mold geographic features (hills, valleys, lakes, etc.) from dough.

• Use twine, twigs, pebbles, flowers and sand to finish the scene (see sketch).

Conversation Suggestions: Each student uses his or her map to briefly retell Bible story it illustrates. You may need to ask questions to help student recall story details. **(And then what did the Levite do? Where were the robbers hiding?)**

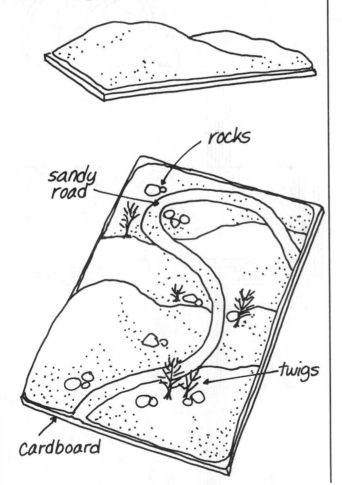

Pebble Friends

Materials: Small flat rocks and pebbles, assorted colored stones (used in aquariums), small wiggle eyes, acrylic paints, paintbrushes, tacky glue. Optional—hot glue gun and glue stick.

Preparation: Wash rocks and pebbles thoroughly. Arrange pebbles and stones in separate piles. Make a sample "Pebble Friend" following instructions below.

Instruct each student in the following procedures:

• Experiment arranging rocks, pebbles and stones together to create a small character.

• Glue pieces together to make character. Try to keep flat sides of stones together.

• Glue on eyes to make a face.

• Use paint to add facial features (see sketch).

Conversation Suggestions: **Does your "Pebble Friend" look like you, a friend or something you imagined? What is something you like about yourself? About a friend? Have you ever told your friend that you appreciate him or her? Our Bible reminds us to *Encourage one another* (see 1 Thessalonians 5:11).**

Paper Jewelry
(A Two-Day Project)

Materials: Lightweight cardboard, pencil, assorted colors of construction paper, waxed paper, scissors, glue, heavy books for weights, coarse sandpaper, varnish or clear acrylic spray, plastic lacing or yarn, awl.

Preparation: Cut several cross patterns from cardboard. With awl, punch a hole in the same place near top of each cross pattern.

Instruct each student in the following procedures:

• Trace cross pattern onto several different colors of construction paper. (Each student should make 15 to 30 crosses.)

• Cut out two or three crosses at a time, making sure each cross is exactly the same size.

• With awl, punch hole in top of each cross.

• Glue all crosses together, stacking one on top of another to make a colorful rainbow effect.

• Make sure all layers are lined up. Wipe off any excess glue.

• Place a piece of waxed paper and then a book on top of the cross to prevent curling while drying. Let dry overnight.

• Sand edges of the cross (see sketch). (Sanding at an angle will reveal the many colorful layers in the cross.)

• Paint front and back of cross with varnish or spray with clear acrylic spray.

• Allow to dry and then string as necklace.

Conversation Suggestions: **Let's think of places in our church building** (in our town) **where we see a cross. Why do you think Christian people like to see a cross? What does a cross remind us of? Why do you think we don't draw Jesus on the cross? We know that Jesus did not stay on the cross. He rose from the dead. Now He is living in heaven.** Listen carefully to students' comments to determine what they understand (or misunderstand) about Jesus' death and resurrection.

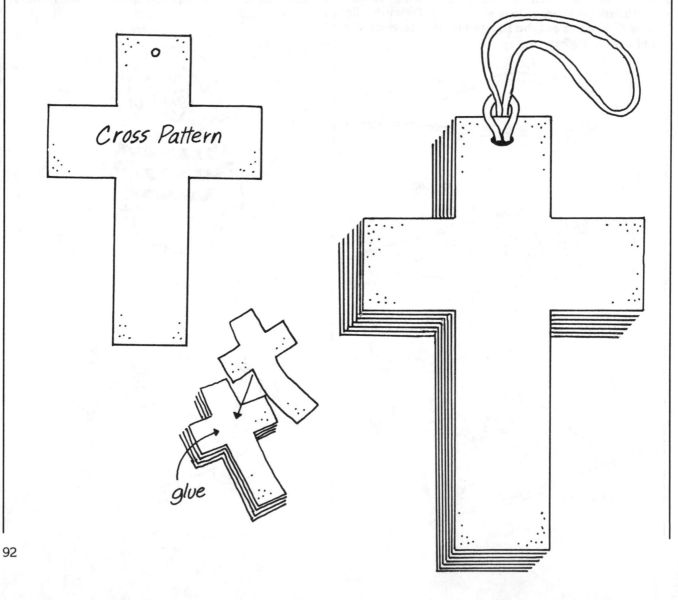

Cross Pattern

glue

Rainbow Plaster
(Two-Day Project)

Materials: Plaster of paris, water, glue, paintbrushes, containers for mixing plaster, spoons, liquid detergent, several colors of household dye (such as food coloring), pencils, cutting tools (nail, file, knives, chisels). For each student—a small foil pan for a mold.

Preparation: None.

Instruct each student in the following procedures:

Day 1:

- Decide on design to carve in order to determine the color sequence of plaster.
- Coat the inside of foil pan mold with liquid detergent.
- Mix three parts plaster of paris with two parts water (to which one color has been added). Stir. Let stand a minute before pouring.
- Pour the first layer of plaster to ⅛ inch thickness.
- Tap sides of mold gently to release any air bubbles.
- When first layer is partially set (firm to touch), mix and pour the second layer (using another color) to about a ¼ inch (.625 cm) thickness. Let set until firm to touch.
- Continue until all layers have been poured (sketch a). The final layer must fill the mold to the desired thickness of the piece. Let dry overnight.

Day 2:

- Remove plaster from mold.
- Mix equal parts of water and glue. Paint the plaster surface with the mixture. Let dry.
- With a pencil, lightly trace a design onto top of plaster ("top" is the side that was at the bottom of mold).
- Use cutting tools to gently scrape design into plaster so the different colors are exposed. The result will be a rainbow effect (sketch b).

Conversation Suggestions: As students work, help them to know their designs do not have to look like anything in particular. **When we make a design that is not a picture of something else, we call it an abstract design. We can see many abstract designs in God's creation. Have you ever seen a design in the clouds? In a stream of water? In jagged rocks on a hillside? You can use your imagination to make an abstract design in your rainbow plaster.**

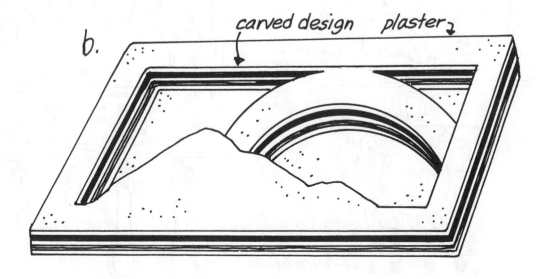

a. *Thin layers of colored plaster* — *foil pan* (side view - cross section)

b. *carved design* *plaster*

Spoon Holder

Materials: Felt (red, green, orange, yellow), glue, scissors, hole punch, tagboard, pencils, felt tip pens. For each student—one Stryofoam box (produce or meat container, about 5 inches [12.5 cm] square), two chenille wires, two 5-inch (12.5-cm) doilies.

Preparation: Using tagboard, make vegetable patterns—one for every two or three students. Cut three sides off Styrofoam container, leaving three short sides and one taller side (sketch a).

Instruct each student in the following procedures:

- Cut chenille wire in half and form loop.
- Poke ends of wire loop through top edge of Styrofoam box and glue in place (sketch b).
- Glue one doily to inside of container.
- Punch four holes in taller side of container (sketch b).
- Cut long chenille wire into four equal sections.
- Insert each piece of wire through a hole.
- Bend top half of each wire flat against container and glue it in place.
- Bend bottom half of wires into hooks (sketch c).
- Trace vegetable patterns onto felt and cut out. (Students may choose which vegetables to make.)
- Arrange felt vegetables on doily and glue in place (sketch c).

Enrichment Idea: Fold second doily in half. Letter the words "Measure Your Kindness Until Overflowing" on the doily. Glue to inside of tall edge of container (sketch d).

Simplification Idea: Pre-cut the felt vegetables for your class. Allow students to choose and arrange them on their doilies.

Conversation Suggestions: **Your spoon holder might be a nice gift for someone. It can be hung in the kitchen with measuring spoons hanging on the hooks. Who would you like to give your spoon holder to? Giving a gift is a good way to show kindness. What are some other ways you can show kindness?**

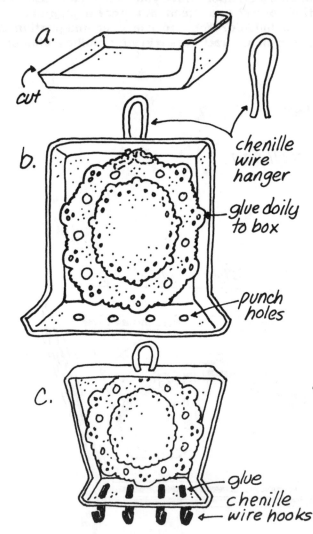

a. cut

b. chenille wire hanger

glue doily to box

punch holes

c. glue chenille wire hooks

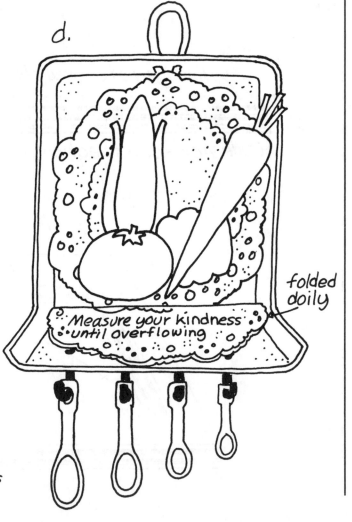

d. folded doily

Measure your kindness until overflowing

Spoon Holder Patterns

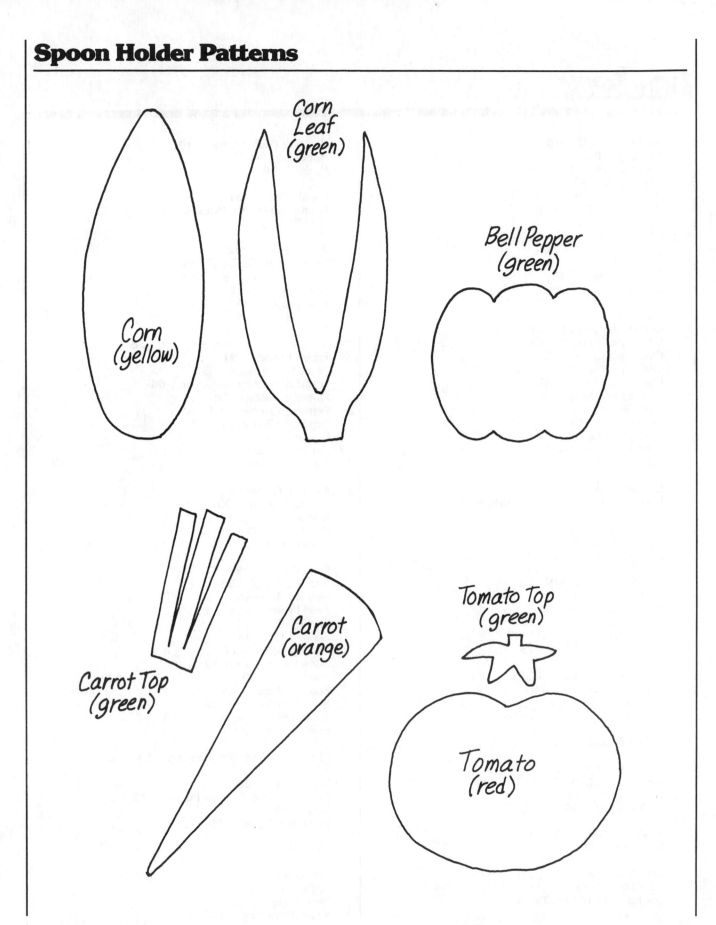

Corn Leaf (green)

Corn (yellow)

Bell Pepper (green)

Carrot Top (green)

Carrot (orange)

Tomato Top (green)

Tomato (red)

Index